T E D D Y
B E A R
ARTIST'S
ANNUAL

Who's Who in Bear Making

Compiled by Rosemary and Paul Volpp,
Donna Harrison and Dottie Ayers

Hobby House Press

Published by

Cumberland,
Maryland 21502

Extra Photographic Credits
Keith C. Allen for Darlene Allen, Robert Buckner for Lynda H. Buckner, William M. Claustre for Donna Claustre, William F. Moser for Vera J. Moser, Christina Neff and Bill McElwain for Maureen McElwain, Ed Eudy for Anniece Summerville, Nancy Bamford for Billee M. Henderson, Richard Herbert for Sandy Williams, Mike Franks for Gloria Franks, Bob Hood for Rhonda Haught, Dottie Ayers for Sue Foskey, Elaine Fujita-Gamble and Laurie Saski, Tony Sibol for Marcia Sibol, Dale L. Imler for Thresa A. Imler, Bill Benson for Anne E. Cranshaw, Tom Bronzino for Barbara Bronzino, Elsa Wolf for Genie Buttitta, Wayne Perry for John Sawyer, Andy Phillips for Kathleen Wallace, Martin E. Howey for Shirley Howey, Jeanette Demanovich for Barbara Koch, John Clarke for Diane Gard, Nicholas Brent for Wendy Brent, Chadwick L. Martin for Carol Martin, Edward C. Salas for Lynn Lumley, Reagan Atkinson for Mary Fran Baldo, Jim Dodson for Sherri Dodson, Michelle Neaves for Mary Neaves, Robert Duvall for Deanna Duvall and Dayla Smoland, David Hertz for Mirian Hertz, David M. Ruegg for Hillary Hulen, Roger Holm for Bev Miller Landstra, Price Policky for Rose Policky, Beverly Port for John Paul Port and Kimberlee Port, George Comito for Janice Comito, Patricia Lyons for Joyce T. O'Sullivan. Michael Gill for Barbara Brown and Serieta Harrell, Robert Cubillas for Corla Cubillas, Peter Wang for Liz Dahle, Don Howard for Suzanne De Pee, David Burbek for Barbara Burbek, Nick Tsai for Tatum Egelin, Tom Wilson for Flore Emory, Brian Maurer for Sandy Fleming, Bill Benson for Donna Hodges, Paul Volpp for Lori Gardiner and Linda Spiegel, R. Keith Donaldson for Pat Johnson, Bob Allen for Doris King, Ken Yoshitomi, Jim Deering, Stewart Schulze for Gloria Rosenbaum, Linda Mullins for Colleen Tipton, Larry McDaniel for Joan Woessner, John Tucker for Paulette Tucker.

Additional copies of this book may be purchased at $14.95
from
Hobby House Press, Inc.
Cumberland, Maryland 21502
or from your favorite bookstore or dealer
Please add $2.25 for postage

Printed in the United States of America

ISBN: 0-87588-341-9

Table of Contents

Table of Contents

Teddy Bear Artists' Annual — An Introduction

First came playthings for children: the rattle, blocks, tinkertoys, pull toys and then the doll. Just after the turn of the century the teddy bear captured the hearts of millions of children and adults. Some say the teddy bear became the most pervasive plaything of the 20th century as it is regarded as a plaything for both girls and boys. In 1906 the media decreed that teddy bears were a fad. Indeed, there have been peaks and valleys in the number of bears brought into the world each year. One immense boost to the popularity of the bear was the 1968 watershed publication, *The Teddy Bear Book* by Peter Bull. Adults used this book to justify the public show of affection for the teddy bear, and the bear world has not been the same since! One might safely say that the teddy bear is for children of all ages.

The teddy bear, through the providence of the adult arctophile, has taken on augmented roles and personalities. Collectors who once were satisfied with collecting teddies made in modest quantities by commercial manufacturers soon yearned for bears made in even smaller numbers and reflecting an even greater variety of roles and personalities. Thus was born the need for the teddy bear artist.

What is a Teddy Bear Artist?

It is the individual artist who totally determines the creation and the personality of the teddy bear through its design, construction, sewing and finishing. The artists' focus their creative talents and imagination to breathe character and life into the bruin. Where separates the teddy bear artist from the designer is the need to utilize his or her skills in producing the teddy bear in final form. By contrast, the designer turns over the details of assembly, construction and finishing to a commercial manufacturing firm.

How Many Bears Does An Artist Make?

The novice bear maker's desire to create teddy bears soon gives way to the realities of repetitive stitching and arduous finishing, added to the challenges of the "I want it now" demands of collectors. Creative people with full imaginations want the challenges that making different models of teddy bears offers. The demands made on bear artists, and their reaction to controlling or channeling these challenges, creates the different degrees of bears: open edition, limited edition, limited production, and one-of-a-kind teddy bears. Let us examine what each type of teddy bear production means to both the teddy bear artist and the collector.

The open edition is a term used for a particular size and design of bear where there are no limitations to the numbers to be produced by the teddy bear artist. The number made of this edition is limited only by the available time and the interest level of the teddy bear artist and the demand of collectors! As collectors have no definition as to numbers or to the time period during which these bears will be made, there is no scarcity and thus supply will nearly always match demand.

A limited edition teddy bear will quote a precise number of bears to be made of a particular size and fabric, with a specific costume and a specific sculptural design for the bear. Sometimes the edition will be differentiated only by the costume styling or the accessory which accompanies the bear. Normally one should expect the limited edition bear to be a number of 250 (ie. 1/250 if this was the first of 250 bears to be produced). For collectors this method of production limitation might produce investment opportunities since there is a fixed supply and no limitation to demand. Thus, when the edition is sold out, the other collectors who wish to purchase these bears may have to pay a premium price for them.

Another less common limitation to numbers produced by the teddy bear artist is the limited production designation. By this a teddy bear artist agrees to fill all orders taken during a specific time period (for example, production can be limited to the calendar year 1990). The teddy bear artist would make the model "to order" and deliver to the sources in a sequence determined by the purchase order date. With this kind of production, unforeseen problems may develop, such as a lack of additional fabrics or materials, which can slow down production by the artist.

A one-of-a-kind teddy bear is the rarest type of offering by a teddy bear artist. The artist would agree to having one, and only one, teddy bear made in a particular fabric, with a particular costume, or in a particular size. The price of such a offering might be high as the artist has to recover his or her development time and efforts from the one model. To the enthusiast this is the ultimate collectible to purchase because it is unique. A prototype made for a commercial firm or made to be replicated by cottage industry workers would qualify as a one-of-a-kind if the prototype was made and finished solely by the teddy bear artist.

What Qualifies a Bear as Being an Original?

A teddy bear artist original bear has to be made wholly from the artist's own design — not from commercial patterns or kits. The design or sculpture, the pattern drafting, the sense of proportion and the finishing of the bear must involve the originality and the artistry of the teddy bear artist.

Let us examine each of these elements in the originality of the bear and appeal to the collector. The design or sculpture of the bear is of paramount importance.

Elongated limbs and humped backs are desirable as they give the bear an antique look. But it is the face that draws on much of the design and sculptural skills of the artist. For it is the face that transmits emotion and mirrors what the collector is looking for in a bear companion.

The pattern drafting must reflect the originality of the artist or the bear is merely an interpretation of another person's design. Involved with the design and sculpture and pattern drafting is a good sense of proportion. For a teddy bear to be salable, there must be a harmony between the bear's theme and each element of the bear which helps the artist to convey the "soul" of the teddy. These elements must compliment one another and not be a distraction from the "look" of the bear.

Of particular importance to the reputation and the "look" of the teddy bear artist are the finishing techniques utilized in finalizing a design. Needlework is primarily used to bring character or life to the teddy bear.

It is our pleasure to bring to your, the reader, a bevy of some of the newest and the best designs being offered to teddy bear collectors today. Bears from all over the world were sought out by Rosemary and Paul Volpp, Donna Harrison and Dottie Ayers for consideration in the first *Teddy Bear Artists' Annual*. Thousands of teddy bears were reviewed and from the collective judgement of these august teddy bear collectors and promoters where chosen the hundreds of different designs which are included. Many of these teddy bear artists will be known to you and there will also be many new faces — both teddy bears and artists. Please be sure to read "How To Use This Book" before starting to maximize the hours of enjoyment that *Teddy Bear Artists' Annual* can bring you. It is arranged geographically for your traveling expeditions either in your armchair or in your car. A handy alphabetical index to teddy bear artists is also included so you can quickly locate your personal favorites. Be sure to contact the teddy bear artist before you visit to assure that they or their studio receive visitors. Teddy bear artists need all of the creative and sewing time they can muster. We give you not only a gallery of teddy bear designs but also feature photographs and short biographies of their creators, to whom this book is dedicated. After all, it is their vivid imaginations, their talents and their hours of trial and error which so greatly enrich our teddy bear collector lives!

Enjoy!

Hobby House Press Publishing Staff

How To Use This Book

The *Teddy Bear Artists' Annual* is planned so that it will be extremely easy to locate any specific bear artist. The book is arranged into seven chapters, geographic regions: Northeast, Southeast, Midwest, Southwest, California, Northwest and Other Countries. The Table of Contents lists the artists alphabetically under each geographic area. At the beginning of each chapter is an alphabetized list of the artists in that region and the page numbers on which they appear. A map of the region also appears on this introductory page.

The index of the book lists the artists alphabetically. In the index the name of the artist, their company name (if any) and address are given. Many teddy bear artists do not have business establishments and work out of their homes. Therefore, no phone numbers are provided. It is recommended that you write to the artist before planning a visit. Look for the teddy bear artists at teddy bear shows and sales.

Northeast

Carol Cavallaro

15" mohair *Heather*.

"This is me — designer, cutter-outer, sewer, stuffer and proud mother of all the teddy bears and teddy bunnies you see here."

15" mohair *Bobby*.

Nancy Lynn Gatto

Limerick Bear

18" mohair *Austin*.

"For many years I have been making...crafts to sell at local craft shows. About four years ago I noticed that people were asking specifically for my teddy bears, which were made from commercial patterns. While attending my first teddy bear show, I decided to try my hand at designing my own patterns. A little over two years ago, I entered my first teddy bear show with my original design acrylic teddies. Now that I have discovered mohair and how marvelous it is to work with, I no longer do the acrylic bears. No matter how many bears I make, each one comes with its own personality."

10½" upholstery mohair *Jester* Bears.

Diane Sherman Turbarg

Bear In The Woods

15" plush *Mindy*.

"I live in Westbrook, Connecticut, with my husband, Ray & daughter Kari. Six years ago I made my first teddy for something to do. After showing my bears to a shop owner in Boston, I was in business. I make bears from 1½" to 24". I am the mother of two and was born in Stockton, California. nia."

9" mohair *My Old Faded Teddy*.

Sue E. Foskey

14" mohair *Money Bear*.

"I began designing teddy bears five years ago after making my first teddy for daughter, Jennifer. Ever since then, I have been designing and making contemporary teddy bears under the trade name of The Nostalgic Bear Co. Some of my special exclusive designs include bears for John Hartford and Reba McEntire. I recently began designing authentic-looking "antique" teddy bears. Each teddy is individually distressed, straw stuffed with antique shoe button type eyes, and dressed in vintage attire. They are sold under the label of The Nostalgic Bear Co.'s Reproductions."

22" mohair *Sailor Bear*.

Margaret F. Viens
Rak-A-Ree-Bos

12" mohair and Merino wool *Calico*.

"**B**eing a full-time teddy bear artist has its physical limitations for me, as I also teach aerobics part-time and am the mother of two small boys. But I do manage to personally create each bear from their original designs to the finishing touches. I then sign, date, number, and name each bear when completed. My bears are called 'Rak-A-Ree-Bos.' The name is an old Maine Yankee expression I learned from my grandfather. It was a term he had for any small animal you might hear, but not see, when out in the woods. The animals that made the noises were the "rakareebos." So, when I started making my own small animals, our family expression seemed to be the perfect name."

9" mohair *Danny*.

Carol-Lynn Rössel Waugh

11" mohair *Bear*.

"**A**s one of the first teddy bear artists in America, I have worked in many media, starting in porcelain and latex, later working in watercolors, and, since 1985, in mohair. I am perhaps best known in the bear world for my writing and photography. My pioneering book, *Teddy Bear Artists: Romance of Making and Collecting Bears* is a classic. As the designer of "Yetta Nother Bear," I now design original bears commercially for two firms: the House of Nisbet in England and Effanbee in the United States and, since 1988, have been offering my original bears, most of them one-of-a-kind, on a very limited basis to collectors."

14" mohair *Hannah*.

Marcia Sibol

Bar Harbor Bear Co.

"I jokingly say 'I was born with a needle in my hand.' As a child I busied myself making doll clothes and by age 10, my own. My first jointed bear, Barnaby, was born in 1982 after years of sewing for people and making soft-sculpture toys. The bears I now design and make range from elegant ladies in hand-beaded lace gowns to children in simple clothes. I do all the work: from research and design to the final stitches. The bears have won numerous prizes and can be seen at hand-selected bear shops as well as the bear shows I attend."

17" mohair *Dearhart*.

Marcia Sibol

11" mohair *The Liberty Girls*.

20" mohair *Lady Aubergine*.

Sherry Hadock

Goldilocks and the Bears

"Having been involved in everything creative all my life, it seems very natural to be making bears for a living, especially since I always wanted a teddy bear as a child — but never had one. All work is done by myself on the bears. All are one-of-a-kind, signed, dated & numbered. I have fully-jointed teddies, 'Huggables,' 'My Honey Drippers,' teddy doorstops & Amish doorstops. At present, all bears are made of synthetic fur, except a few that are made of mink or mouton. Each bear is named and all names are used only once, in order to keep them one-of-a-kind."

Caramel Cutey.

Durae Allen

"The first Lil' Honey Bear came to life in 1985. Since that time I have combined my creative talent and designing knowledge to create a teddy bear business with the support of my husband. He suggested that I leave my management job and enter the world of teddy bear artists. I enjoy designing and love to make small editions or one of a kind bears. I work on bears seven days a week. When I'm not working with my hands sewing, stuffing, and finishing I am thinking of new designs. Because the demands have exceeded the amount of bears that I can produce, I am working on a line of German manufactured bears whereby I will complete the faces and do all the trimming."

21" mohair *Sabrina*.

14" mohair *Karri Asleep/Awake*.

Durae Allen

4" to 7" mohair teddies.

Thresa A. Imler

My Best Friends

13" mohair *Barclay*.

"I have always had a love for teddy bears and stuffed toys. For the past three years, I have collected artist's bears and experimented with my own patterns. In 1987, I began working with Darryl Shachat of Bears From Birnam Woods, where I gained experience in designing and constructing quality teddy bears. By April of 1988, I felt I had a design other collectors would like and began 'My Best Friends.' Currently, I have nine unique teddy bears in three different sizes, each with a personality of its own. I hope my bears bring enjoyment to everyone."

13" mohair *Clownish Antics*.

Alice Ann Liles

20" *Santa Claus Bear*.

"I had always adored my friend's antique teddy bear that sat in an old-time chair in her dining room and because I knew I'd never find one like it, I set out to make one myself. My first bears are funny and I have kept and loved them, but I have improved their 'character' over the years. Friends had asked if I would make bears for them and one particular friend who owned an antique shop asked if I would make bears for her shop window at Christmas. Thus began my career in teddy bear making."

20" *Overall Bear*.

Donna Low

10" mohair *Davy*.

"After collecting Steiff animals for ten years I discovered artist bears and began collecting them. Five years ago I decided to make my own bear, thinking it couldn't be too difficult. The first bear was a disaster and I wouldn't go near my sewing machine for six months! When I finally tried again the results were better. I changed my pattern many times before I got the cute, cuddly look I was trying for. Now my biggest problem is parting with my bears because I fall in love with every one!"

T.J.

Laura Turner

Windsor Cottage Crafts

16" *Bear Heart*, 6" *J.T.*, and 16" *Tattered Teddy*, all mohair.

"My bear making began eight years ago with a small corduroy teddy and has grown into a full time vocation. Working in German mohair and old fabrics, combined with my love of antique dolls and toys, has influenced my designs to take on a warm, nostalgic appearance. Joining all the teddies are also original mohair rabbits and hand-painted cloth dolls created to appeal to the teddy bear collector and antique lover."

24" mohair *Hippity*.

Debra L Bedwell

D'Bears

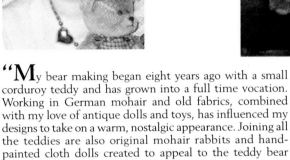

Lambswool bunnies.

"The D'Bears animals are very special little critters. They are hand-made using unusual genuine curley lambswool, mink and various furs. I place a loving message in the heart of each bear, giving them their own individual and precious spirit! I started making bears, bunnies and lambs in 1985. I had made a little rabbit for a friend and had such a response from those who saw it that I took a few orders. Since then, I have sold to Neiman-Marcus, Bloomingdales and many fine and unique stores."

Lambswool *Emily*.

Sara R. Phillips

"I share my life & bears with my husband, George, and two year old son, Jimmy, both big supporters of my work! Other interests include miniatures, dance, and theater. I also teach special education. My bear career started in early 1981, when I couldn't find good miniature reproductions of antique-type jointed bears for a mini teddy bear shop I was making. As a result, I decided to try making some myself! I've always liked miniatures, teddies, and creating things, so the three just sort of naturally combined! I especially enjoy putting lots of details into my bears."

Bear with Paw Puppet.

1¾" velour *Clown with clown paw puppet.*

Pink compact bear and blue perfume bear.

Nutcracker Bear.

Anne E. Cranshaw

5" mohair *Eliot*.

"I made my first bear in January 1984 and was so pleased with the results that I made him a vest and tie and he was known as 'Papa Bear.' He has since acquired a pair of glasses and a new name: *E. Willoughby*. I joined The Teddy Bear Club of Des Moines and discovered that bears are even more fun when shared. I met Charlotte Joynt and Steve Schutt at one of the club meetings. I still remember the bear making tips and ideas we shared that evening. In November 1984 I did my first show: The Des Moines Teddy Bear Exhibit. I sold many bears, took orders for more and even won the Best Handmade Bear Contest. I was hooked!"

11½" mohair *Mary Helen*.

Elva Hughes

Barrington Bears

12" Merino wool *Bonsai*.

"The start of bear making came in 1978 with a store bought pattern. These designs were changed or discarded as my skills improved. It is still a challenge to follow thru with a new idea. I really enjoy making bears with a funny theme and to watch the smiles of adults and the giggles of children."

10" mohair "Masquerade" clown.

Lois Gile Laverty

Gile Teddy Bears™

12" and 17" plush "Mugsy" bears.

"I have been designing and making teddy bears for at least five years and I am a member of the American Teddy Bear Artists Guild and The Good Bears of the World. I also do teaching and lecturing about bears and have been in several teddy bear shows around New England. Prior to this, I did dressmaking and tailoring part time, while I worked as a data entry operator. None of these professions are important to me now as I have found my true identity in being a teddy bear artist and designer. I use only the highest quality materials available and I strive for perfection."

17" plush *Randy*.

Joyce A. Miller
Bears & Other Quilted Crafts

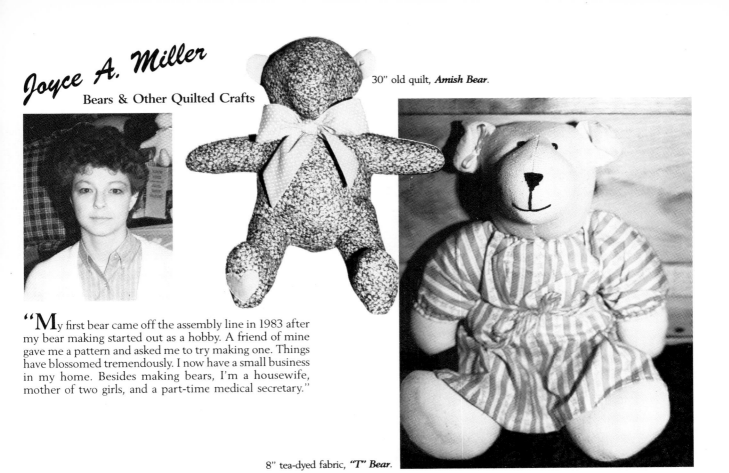

30" old quilt, *Amish Bear*.

"**M**y first bear came off the assembly line in 1983 after my bear making started out as a hobby. A friend of mine gave me a pattern and asked me to try making one. Things have blossomed tremendously. I now have a small business in my home. Besides making bears, I'm a housewife, mother of two girls, and a part-time medical secretary."

8" tea-dyed fabric, *"T" Bear*.

Barbara Bronzino and JoAnn Brown
B&J Originals

14" fur *Washday Mama and Baby* (4").

Barbara Bronzino and JoAnn Brown.

"**B**arbara & I have been working together for over 20 years and both of us are self-taught in the field of soft sculpture. We design different patterns to go with ideas for our character bears. Our bears range in size from 4" to 28". Some of the outfits are made from adult old clothes and scaled down to fit the bears. Our characters are repeated but because of the outfits they are always 'one of a kind.' Making bears has been very enjoyable for both of us and has led to B&J Originals."

17" mohair *Pops* and 8" *Grandbear*.

Dee Hockenberry

"**I** am a contributing writer to *Teddy Bear and friends®* magazine and author of *Bearers of Memories* and *Collectible German Animals Value Guide*. I am also a bear artist and a dealer in collectible Steiff animals and teddies."

11" mohair *Jester*.

Dee Hockenberry

11" mohair *Jester*.

Carolyn Jacobsen

8½" upholstery fabric *Monday's Child*.

"**F**ifteen years ago my husband, Bill, and I bought our first old bear. After years of collecting, I began making bears with commercial patterns but never quite got the look I wanted. I studied my old bears, calendars, books, other people's bears and sketched what appealed to me most. Armed with a strong desire to create, I put together a pattern. We laughed! After much effort the first saleable teddy of my own design came to be. I especially love to work with vintage fabrics for an old classic look."

11½" mohair *Buster*.

Genie Buttitta

Genie B's Bears

"Collecting and restoring bears has been a part of my life for ten years. After making a few bears as gifts, I was in the bear business overnight. I have enjoyed judging teddy bear contests and doing three local T.V. programs on bears. Creating bears from morning till night isn't like work to me, it's exciting. My rewards are seeing happy smiling faces of those who choose my bears for their own collection. The teddy is a warm childhood friend: I love being a part of this love and friendship by making bears."

17" imitation persian lamb *Julius C. Bearmaker*.

Genie Buttitta

8½" mohair **Scrubby Teddy**.

8½" mohair **Trashy Teddy**.

Kathy Nearing

Little Seesie.

"**O**ver two years ago I decided I wanted a teddy. Since I didn't know it was all right for a grandmother to buy herself a bear, I decided to make one. Naturally, I couldn't stop with one bear so making teddies has become a most enjoyable way of life."

Clyde.

Terry Hayes

Pendleton's Teddy Bears

20" mohair *Camille* and 14" mohair *Sassy*.

"I started making plush teddy bears 5-1/2 years ago when I was pregnant with my daughter. I have a degree in Nuclear Medicine and decided to stay home and be a mother. After learning about the history of teddy bears and attending conventions, I started designing my own patterns. For the past 3-1/2 years I've been making mink and genuine fur bears. I do a lot of bears for individuals made from their grandma's mink stole or mother's coat: something to remember them by. I'm hooked on bears."

20" mohair *Victoria*.

Maggie Iacono

4" mohair *Jennifer*.

"I grew up in Minnesota and settled here in Pennsylvania after a few years of teaching elementary school in Australia. Eight years ago I began making and selling cloth dolls. This quite naturally slipped into making bears as well. I couldn't believe the interest in these first few attempts. So I made more and became hooked on them ever since. What kept my excitement in these lovable creatures was all the different colors and textures of fur that can be found. My favorite thing is to see the "spark of life" that can come to the bear when different costumes and/or accessories are added."

10" mohair *Emily*.

Joyce Reichard

Bears By Joyce

10" plush fur *Billy*.

"**I** was born in Southbridge, MA in 1943, and moved to Milton, PA, in 1967. Married with two children, I wanted to establish a small business at home while the children were in school. It began with sewn crafts and Raggedy Ann dolls. I began making Teddy Bears five years ago. I attend five to six craft shows per year, sell from my home and a few select shops in Pennsylvania."

10" plush fur *Bashful Becky*.

John Sawyer

15" fur *Kimbearly*.

"**I** am a computer programmer by profession and a bear-a-holic by preference. My wife, Donna Marie, and I started collecting bears several years ago. Bearly two years ago, I became interested in making bears and, with Donna's help, created Bears by Chon, Inc. The 'Chon' comes from the Pennsylvania Dutch pronunciation of 'John.' My bears are made from either acrylic fur or mohair and are fully jointed. Most of my bears range from 13" to 17" in height. I was born in Washington, D.C., and lived in Greece, Taiwan, and Minneapolis-St. Paul before moving to Pennsylvania in 1975."

13" fur *Preston*.

Patricia Fici

Trishka's Treasures

"My initiation into the world of teddy bear making took place about four years ago when my children were in pre-school. In a rather desperate effort to silence their cries for 'a guinea pig just like our school pet,' I created *Giggles* and *Twiggles*. Made from a variety of furs and containing squeakers, these minimal-care, non-odoriferous guinea pigs were well received by not only my own children but by their classmates and their classmates parents as well. I was soon working to fulfill requests for other animals. Ultimately I worked up to teddy bears as my childhood love of stuffed animals was revived by that of my children. I use only my own designs for the bears and their costumes. I do work entirely alone which consequently limits my annual production. As my work has progressed and matured, I more and more frequently envision my bears as sculptures, albeit with somewhat fluid natures given their ability to change poses."

12" mohair *...and Ladies of the C'ub.*

12" and 8" fur *Ready for Bed*.

Patricia Fici

15" mohair *But Woman's Work is Never Done*.

24" alpaca mohair *Pierre Lapin*.

Edda Seiple

16" shag *Chester* and 12" German plush *Sammy*.

"It seems I was born with a needle in my hand. I love to take on a new challenge. For years I made cloth dolls. All my bears were given to me as gifts. I decided to make a teddy when my granddaughter was born. I struggled for years before I came up with the first design that resembled what I had in mind. Now I love making teddy bears, and depending on the type of bear I'm working on, I use both mohair and acrylic fabrics. I enjoy experimenting, and always am on the look-out for unusual fabric finds."

14" mohair *Denis*, 18" mohair *Belinda* and 17" wavy wool *Arthur*.

Gary and Margaret Nett

Bears by Nett

"The root of Bears by Nett began some 35 years ago. My mother, Margaret, sewed professionally and still found time to make stuffed animals. The designing and making of Nett bears is now a joint effort between my mother and myself. I started making bears in 1983, after losing a job in the construction field. My inspiration came through my mother who is a master at her craft. A lot of my design experience through architectural construction, has prompted a quest for perfection in detail, making it an inherent part of Bears by Nett philosophy. Consequently, every new bear design is an exercise in self-improvement."

18" mohair *Black Bear*.

18" mohair *Confederate Infantry Major* and *Southern Belle*.

10" mohair **Ruben**.

Kathleen Wallace

Stier Bears

15" mohair **Ruthie**.

"**I** have been making bears for five years. The first ones were just craft bears. The more I looked around for old bears I realized the need for good vintage-type bears for people who did not want to pay the price for antiques. In 1987 I decided to make a business from my hobby. My husband, Jim, and I now make the bears on a full time basis and love every minute of our new venture."

22" mohair **Wally**.

Southeast

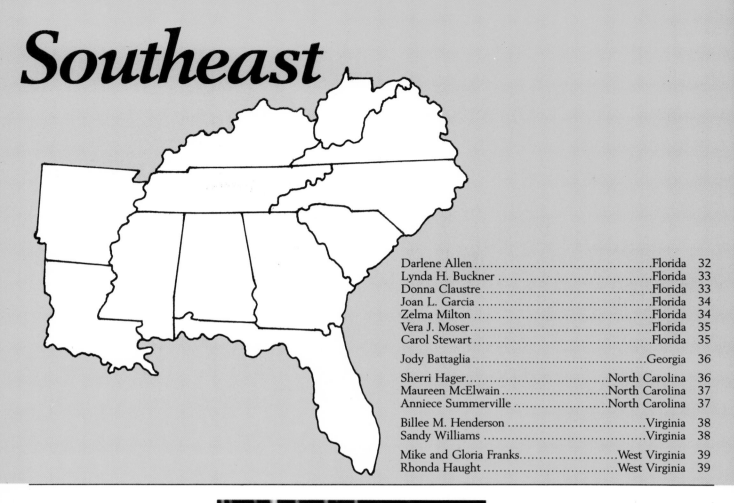

Darlene Allen

Raspbeary Bears

10" distressed mohair *Raspbeary*.

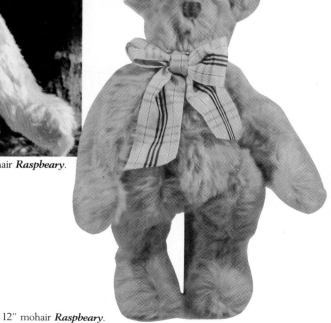
12" mohair *Raspbeary*.

"Cincinnati, Ohio is my birthplace and hometown. I married my college boyfriend, Keith, who joined the Navy. After receiving my degree in business administration I joined him to travel across the states. During those years I taught children with reading disabilities and taught an art study course for others in Hawaii. But my love of art and writing stayed at the forefront. I made things — dolls, quilts, and pillows. And when I was too cheap to buy a name brand bear Christmas stocking, I decided to make my own. What evolved was a jointed Raspbeary bear with story book and a self-taught bear artist."

Lynda H. Buckner

The Incredible Teddy™

14" mohair *Honey Baby*.

"The special sense of family and love that I was brought up in is reflected into each little bear. I began sewing at the age of five. My grandmother taught me to sew little clothes for my dolls. It was not until 1983 that I began my successful teddy bear business. My award winning bears all reflect the meticulous attention each receives. The bears range in size from tiny six inch bears to thirty inch character bears which are made to suit each customer's fancy and special needs. Some are very sophisticated and made of fine mohair, alpaca, velvets, and real furs, while others are constructed out of antique quilts and upholstery materials."

7" alpaca *Elizabeth Ann*.

Donna Claustre

Original Bucktooth Bear

15" synthetic *Bucktooth*.

"After graduation it was my fondest desire to study to be a fashion designer — this was not to be, business college was to prevail. After eighteen years of working, marriage, one child, and retirement in 1980 I finally had time to follow my love for designing. Having collected dolls and bears, my interest naturally turned in this direction and my first creation *Original Bucktooth Bear* was born. A whole new and wonderful world opened to me and my family. We have so much fun in this special world. For us, bears truly mean love."

16" German plush *Precious*.

Joan L Garcia

13" acrylic *Country Bear*.

"**A**s a new mother, I wanted to do something that would let me be at home with my son, provide some income, and satisfy my creative needs. I have sewn since I was about eight, and always wanted to make a bear. It took me a while but after making my first bear in 1983 for my son, friends placed orders, and I expanded to craft shows and a few stores. I make various dressed bears, and a lot of special orders."

13" acrylic *Elizabeth* and *Barnett Bearrington.*

Zelma Milton

Z & J Enterprises

17" Royal plush *Couch Buddies*.

"**I** bought my first Teddy in 1975 and in 1984 I designed my first bear. People seeing my bears said I should be selling, not collecting. In 1987 I started Z & J Enterprises. I have been in arts and crafts all my life. In 1971 I started a craft business in North Carolina. I designed jewelry and Christmas decorations from all varieties of eggshells. I moved to Florida in 1975 and continued until 1977. At that time I was in an automobile accident. The road to recovery has been long. It's nice to be back in the world of design and creation, especially teddy bears."

17" Royal plush *Daddy's Little Girl.*

Vera J. Moser

3¼" synthetic *Corduroy*.

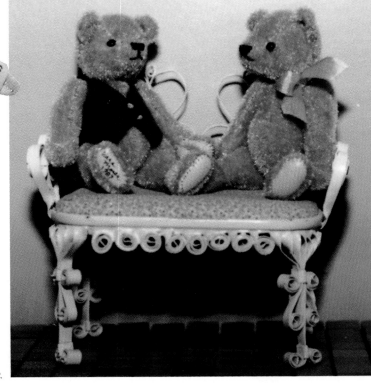

"**M**y creative endeavors started as a child living in a small town in Wyoming. Through the years much time was spent on creative projects in many art forms. I studied needlepoint, ceramics and oil painting. After retirement my husband and I moved to Florida. I became interested in miniatures and more particularly the world of small bears! All my art forms are now encompassed into one — my miniature bears and accessories."

2¾" synthetic *Quiet Moment*.

Carol Stewart

2¼" velvet *Diane*.

"**I** was born 'Christmas Carol' 12/28/49 in Indiana of German and English ancestry. Married to an Irishman, with three grown daughters, I now live in Stuart, Florida. I built my first dollhouse in 1982 and started making miniature toys, specializing in wood carved puppets and teddy bears. I was voted in as artisan member of the International Guild of Miniature Artisans in 1985. Member of the National Association of Miniature Enthusiasts and Stuart Miniature Club. With no formal training, I can only assume that my ability must come from a good mix of genes and a wee bit 'o magic!''

2¼" velvet *Larry*.

Jody Battaglia

Beary Best Friends™

10" acrylic *Mr. Roosevelt*.

"I have been making and dressing bears for ten years now. I specialize in smaller dressed bears. I am 37 years old, and married with two sons. The boys have grown up with bear making and it is a real family project."

13" acrylic *Crackerjack Joe*.

Sherri Hager

18" synthetic *Catawba Cub*.

"I have been involved in arts and crafts since I was a child, coming from a very creative family. My grandmother and aunt both made soft dolls and stuffed animals and I first started sewing by making doll clothes from fabric scraps. I started making teddy bears and dolls four years ago and one of the things I enjoy most is creating their outfits!"

18" synthetic *Alice* and *Teddy Roosevelt*.

Maureen McElwain

8" mohair *Sarah* and *Christopher*.

"I'm a wife, mother of two teenagers, a banker plus a bear artist. I've been making bears seriously for almost four years. I have a small collection of bears plus some that I've made and just couldn't part with. I have a great respect for antique bears and love to go on bear hunts searching for that special one. I love bears and antiques together and try to find antique eye-glasses, beaded purses, cameras, hats etc. to use as accessories for the bears. I'm a member of ATBAG and I'm looking forward to St. Louis in '89. I'm hooked on bear shows already — having met the nicest and most interesting people."

12" mohair *Izaac Walton*.

Anniece Summerville

27" acrylic *Baby Smiley*.

"As a craftsman, adopting classic patterns to create unique personalities and varieties of antique-style teddy bears with jointed arms, legs, and heads has been fun and challenging. For many years I have enjoyed crafts of all kinds, but making stuffed animals has become the most interesting. Excitement and public interest in quality collectible bears persuaded me to concentrate my talents in this area. With a friend, also a bear craftsman, I have exhibited at numerous regional shows, as well as the "1987 Magic of Teddy Bears." I look forward to future exhibits in other regions of the country."

13" acrylic *Precious*.

Billee M. Henderson

19" mohair *Mary Ann*.

"After graduation from the University of Maryland as a clothing and textile major, I spent the following years as a Navy wife, sewing for myself, home(s), gifts and five children. I made my first jointed bear in 1984: *Hamish* in a Henderson kilt for a son born in Scotland. Also born was a "bear obsession" that continues with more ideas than time, as I produce the entire bear from first the idea to the final touches."

17" mohair *Bearnard*.

Sandy Williams

2" ultrasuede teddies.

"I love to make tiny teddy bears — the smaller the better. My dressed teddies are inspired by old clothed bears. All of my two inch and under bears (smallest 5/8") are completely hand sewn — approximately 28 stitches an inch and are made of ultrasuede. Teddy bears, dolls, gardening, quilts, country furniture and raising two teenage sons complete my life."

3/4" to 2" ultrasuede teddies.

Mike and Gloria Franks

by Goose Creek

"We began our bear making careers creating soft muslin dolls which were sold through a variety of different outlets. After attending doll and bear shows we began to notice we were becoming more and more attached to the teddies at the shows, particularly to the more traditional looking bears. We were both collectors of dolls and now bears, so, with our creativity and sewing skills, the progression to bear making came quite naturally. It has been six years since we began creating traditional looking teddies. We have added many new designs to our line of Goose Creek Bears, some still traditional and some totally different."

14" mohair *Dudley*.

14" alpaca *Sonny* and *Sis*.

22" mohair *Cub*.

Rhonda Haught

Maul and Paw Bears

"Maul and Paw Bears' is somewhat of a novelty in my hometown, in that serious bear collecting is an uncommon hobby in Northern West Virginia. Consequently, when I wanted an old-fashioned bear I couldn't find one. So I made *Victor*, who had to have glasses, not because he was nearsighted, but because he was 'lopsided'! Designing *Victor* ignited my passion for bears. When I found my first copy of *Teddy Bear and friends*® I was excited and amazed to find a new world of teddy bear people. I placed an ad and have since sold many bears in the U.S. and in Canada."

22" mohair *Ezeliel*.

Midwest

Sherry Baloun

Bitte Schoen Bears

17" mohair *Lucinda*.

"I have been a collector and admirer of antique and artist bears for six years. Five years ago my mother and I opened Gigi's Dolls and Sherry's Teddy Bears in Niles, Illinois. We travel and do shows all across the country. My bear making started in 1986 when I wanted to do something different for my parents anniversary. So I made a pair of jointed bears dressed in anniversary finery. After that I started designing and making bears of acrylic, wools and mohair. I love taking extra time for finishing touches because it's exciting to see the little personalities each bear takes on."

21" mohair *Rosealinda*.

Gary Lee Phillips

15" acrylic **Hare Odotus**.

"I am a former computer programmer who has been interested in teddy bears all my life. I recently retired from my corporate position to devote full time efforts to writing and the fiber arts, including weaving, spinning, and lace making as well as teddy bear design. I share a large house in Chicago with a friend who does stained glass work, and also with several hundred bears."

12" acrylic **Sandy MacBruin**.

12" ultrasuede and sheared Canadian otter **Ollie**.

Judith Swanson
Fur Real Bears

"My appreciation of natural furs prompted the creation of a bear so that I could enjoy not only my new bear friend but also admire his fur. Friends liked my bear and asked for their own. Each bear is unique and enhanced by variations in color, textures and lengths of hair. They come in a wide selection of furs, but none can be reproduced exactly. Thirty years experience in design and constructing clothing has been beneficial in creating bears, but this is so much fun! If there was no market for another bear, I would continue to create more, because I love it."

12" Australian blush **Peaches 'n Cream**.

Mary Haggard

Haggard Huggables

9" synthetic fur *Chauncey*.

12½" synthetic fur *Chadwick*, 10½" synthetic *Chelsea*.

"I began designing and making teddy bears in 1986 and my first bears were sold two weeks before Christmas '86. They've kept me pretty busy ever since. Although I have a national and international reputation as an Arabian Horse artist I create bears to fill in the slow times (painting). However, recently the bears have kept me busy much more than the paintings!"

Cynthia Powell

Bearly Bears

1¾" *Clown Bear*, 1¾" *Ballerina Bear*.

1¾" *Open Mouth Bear*, 1¾" *Basic Bear*, 1¾" *Muff Bear with tiny bear muff*.

"I have been fascinated by miniatures since I was a child. When my parents traveled they would bring me back tiny objects to play with, many of which I still have. They are little treasures. I feel the same about my little bears. When I became interested in teddy bears in 1986, it was the miniature bear variety that especially captured my attention. I studied books on making large bears then I began to shrink the process to miniature size. I am also an animal lover. I feel protective about the wildlife in my environment. I have a bachelor's degree in fine arts and have explored many art media but I think these bears will hold my attention a long time. I am also a graduate gemologist and design jewelry by profession."

Sayuri "Saki" Romerhaus

Romerhaus Creations

*Front row: 4" **Brüta** holding 2" **Anna**, 5½" **Gretel**. Back row: left; 8" German Merino wool **Gretchen Edelweiss**, 11" honey Merino wool **Wilhelmina HoneyWunsch**, caramel-brown mohair **Rebecca Romerhaus Karmel WunschBear**.*

"I was born an American citizen in Yokohama, Japan, to an American soldier and Japanese mother. At age two, they left Japan and lived in Germany and France for six years. I am self-taught in the arts and thank my Japanese and American ancestors for any talent I possess. My mother taught me well before her death when I was eight. My artistic talent was evident from an early age. I created my first bear in 1982. Richard and I live in Evansville, Indiana, in a house filled with teddy bears, books, antiques, herbs, flowers and whatever!"

Pamela Wooley

Wooley Bear Cottage

"I am 30 years old, married and have one son. My undergraduate degree is in Fine Arts. I have been creating teddies for five years. Each is an original — made solely by myself. My trademark is padded ears. It takes eight to ten hours to make each ted (without clothing). My workmanship and materials are the highest quality and superior. Faces and expression are my utmost concern and many hours are taken to painstakingly hand trim each teddy. I have been an antique collector for over 12 years and I add many small antique accessories to the teddies."

12" mohair **Hannah**.

17" mohair **Baxter**.

Bonnie Windell

Windlewood

"I was born in Evansville, Indiana, and have lived there all of my life. I have been collecting dolls and stuffed animals since childhood. I began sewing when I was nine, making clothes for my collection. A vocal music major for 3½ years, I left college to marry Brad, my husband of 13 years. We have five children, three boys and two girls, and live in the woods on 26 acres. Always an animal lover, I also raise purebred dogs and dairy goats."

Winsome, Demi-Bear, Wee Bear, mohair

Button, Squeaky and *Keevey.*

Squeaky, 7" *Demi-Bear,* 5½" *Wee Bear.*

14" mohair *Wistful,* 9" mohair *Winsome.*

Rafferty, Natty, Katie and *Arthur.*

Bonnie Windell

Applejack with jug and apples.

Nan Wright

Old Tyme Toys & Treasures

26" synthetic fur *Sweet William*.

"I am a Des Moines native with a background in art and photography, who made my first bear in 1971 as a Christmas present for my daughter. In 1978, after the birth of my second child, I turned my hobby into a full time business. My many original designs include open-mouth bears and bears with leather claws. Several of my bears have won top awards on the national as well as the local level, including Golden Teddy Awards in 1987 and 1988. I am one of the founding members of the Iowa Teddy Bear Maker's Guild."

Steve Schutt

"**I** am an Iowa native who turned 17 years of puppet construction skills toward making teddy bears in 1980. My first bears were made for the antique collectors market, later bears for interior or country decorating markets, and in 1985 I started producing bears for the American artist bear collector. I am most proud of an 1987 Golden Teddy Award and three Artists' Choice awards (1986, 1987, 1988) from my peers in the American Teddy Bear Artists Guild."

34" mohair *Victoria Anne*.

Steve Schutt

26" mohair **Cornelious**.

24" mohair **Scruffy**.

Linda Beckman

"I am a Michigan artist who began my career as a doll designer-maker. A teddy pattern was purchased and a few were constructed to place among the dolls for display and the public just seemed to gravitate to the bears. Much frustration and many pattern changes have brought forth a bear with classic looks, an absolutely wonderful face and sweet smile. The exciting part of bear artistry for me is designing the perfect costume. Using rich colors in taffetas, velvets and vintage lace, the beauty and personality of each bear is brought forth."

15" mohair **Cordelia,** 15" mohair **Sarah-Linda,** 15" mohair **Lydia Lyna.**

Laura Caruso

The Country Bear

Serenity.

Marantha the Peddler.

"I began designing and creating antique-style teddy bears in 1982. My love for country and antiques led my designs to look 19th century. I am accomplished at every form of colonial needlework and have put this experience into my bears. All are original designs, with emphasis on detail and facial expression to give each bear his own unique personality. Costumes are fashioned after 19th century designs, again, with emphasis on detail. I use antique fabrics, laces, trims; aged and homespun fabrics; and antique shoe button eyes. In 1988, my bear, *Hannah* was chosen to appear on the 1989 Bialosky Teddy Bear Calendar."

Lynne Flukes

Heavenly Bears

11½" mohair *Lilac*.

"I have been making bears since 1983. I began, hoping to create a bear that reminded me of the bear of my childhood. Once started, I found it impossible to stop. Bears are a creative outlet for me. I come from a very artistic family, and this seems to fulfill a need. I also enjoy being the source of love they seem to bring to collectors. I can't imagine not making teddy bears."

Distressed mohair bear.

Jenny Krantz

14" mohair *T-Kayo-Boxer Bear*.

"Teddies started out to be a hobby then grew to be a loving and strong bond that I developed with them. Bear making then became a full-time business. In our home and business we have a favorite saying: 'There's always room for one more.' I am married with three children, 11 grandchildren and thousands of furry children. What a rewarding work to be in! I love it ."

14" American fur *Chetta*.

Ann Kynion

Beana Bears

Mohair *Posey Bear*.

Plush fur *Madame Bearina*.

"I have spent most of my adulthood in the Ozarks. I am married, have three children, Brenna, Casey and Brian. I have always been creative, but making and selling teddy bears is my first business venture. I helped a friend get started in a business, then called Classic Creations. Due to shifting family situations and a large demand for teddy bears, I struck out on my own and started my own company called Beana bears. Each is handmade, and by creating my unique one-of-a-kind bears it is one of the most rewarding aspects of the bear business. Another is the opportunity to meet the people who take my bears home. I have been featured in articles and magazines and was also included in the local PBS television station's program called *Ozarks Magazine*."

Terry & Doris Michaud

Carrousel by Michaud

"We are known for our handcrafted teddy bears under the Carrousel by Michaud label. Collecting antique teddy bears led us to designing and producing award-winning teddy bears, including our most popular Museum Recreation series. Our teddies are sold in leading shops throughout the United States, and in shops in England and Australia. In addition to bear making, we have authored three books: *Bears Repeating, Stories Old Teddies Tell; How To Make and Sell Quality Teddy Bears; Teddy Tales, Bears Repeating Too;* and write a regular column titled "Bears Repeating" in *Teddy Bear and friends* magazine."

The Old Man Bear.

Terry & Doris Michaud

7" arcylic plush **Doris Purse Bear.** 19" mohair **Terry's Bear.**

13" **Baby Edward,** 18" **Sir Edward II,** 27" **Sir Edward III,** acrylic plush.

Janet Reeves

Hug-A-Bear

13½" ultrasuede, mohair **Lavender 'N Lace.**

10½" ultrasuede, mohair **Country Blue** and **Country Rose.**

"I live in an ideal setting for making bears, as my home is nestled in the woods of rural Midland in Michigan, where I create bears with all the traditional characteristics of old teddies. I especially pay close attention to the fine detail of each bear. I first began making bears in January of 1985. It took several months of research, trial and error, and quite a few laughs, before I created what I call my first 'satisfactory teddy'. Soon after, my bears were sold in shops under the name of Hug-A-Bear. Today Hug-A-Bears can be found in shops across the country, in Australia, and also at shows throughout the year. My bears have been the recipient of numerous awards and ribbons. What I enjoy most about bear making is meeting collectors and sharing the satisfaction that my bears give to other people."

Nancy Crowe

"Having a lifelong interest in the field of arts and crafts, it seemed natural to move in this direction as a means to stay home with small children. I designed my first Rabbit in 1985 and "Pearls" was born. All "Pearls" are my original designs and handcrafted using the highest quality materials."

15" mohair *The Muffin Man*, 11" mohair *The Nanny*.

Nancy Crowe

15" mohair *The Peddler*.

13" mohair *Father Christmas*.

Gloria Adams

The Bearfoot Bear

13" mohair *J.B. (Just Bear)*.

12" white Merino wool *A Bear in Sheep's Clothing*.

"I live in a wooded section of Northeast Ohio with my husband, two teenagers, and lots of teddy bears. Making the bears has given me a creative outlet that has helped get me through some stressful times. There's just something about a teddy bear that makes you smile all the way down to your soul; sharing that with others makes life just a little bit better."

Debbie Kesling

Granny's Locket

"Sincerity and aliveness...That's what I strive for in my bear making. When I struggled making my first teddy (a kit) in 1983, I never imagined that one day my bears would find homes all over the world! I prefer to create bears in mohair and traditional fabrics, but occasionally use old and unusual fabrics when I can find them. Antique shoe button eyes are a must, and each bear comes with an antique or appealing trinket of some sort. All of my bears are classically styled, with humpback and long arms, but are tempered with a touch of whimsy."

13" mohair, ultrasuede *Zowie*, 13" alpaca, ultrasuede *Tharkin*, 13" coat lining, ultrasuede *Kes*.

Debbie Kesling

15" mohair *Aunt Elderbeary*.

13" mohair *Terwilliger*.

The Ohio River Bear Company

Susan Baker

13" *Candy*, 15" *Ned*.

"I'm a former photographer turned teddy bear maker. I'm still not quite sure how it happened but I'm glad it did! I've been in business almost a year. I am married, have four children, and I live in a big, old brick house in the small town of Middleport, Ohio."

10" *Robin*, 10" *Dylan*.

Betsy Reum

Bears-in-the-Gruff

"I am a graduate of Michigan State University with a degree in clothing and textiles. In 1981, I chose the craft business as a creative outlet and means of staying home with my young sons. After five years of refining a commercial pattern bear with original costuming, desire to create unique and original designs grew. In 1986 the first mohair bear, *Toby* was born. Several traditional teddy designs have led to the newer unique characters and limited editions which now represent my company, 'Bears-in-the-Gruff.'"

15" mohair *Prescott,* 7" mohair *Tinker,* 14" mohair *Priscilla.*

Betsy Reum

11" mohair *Parlor Maid*.

15" mohair *Puppeteer*.

Jan Bonner

Modacrylic fur *Night Time Bear*.

Mohair *Court Jester*.

"I am a graduate of Ohio State University in Home Economics. A strong background in sewing and art courses during graduate school were the basis of formal training that taught me the critical basic skills. Upon the arrival of my oldest child in 1976, children's toys caught my imagination. While researching, old bears, styles were formulated and techniques learned. Awards have been received throughout the State of Ohio including Best of Show at the Canton Art Institute and the Ohio State Fair. Recently the Ohio Designer Craftsmen Enterprise has chosen my line to represent in their Arts Marketing Program. I feature my various needlecraft skills in the bear's clothing, this is proving to be 'a fun outlet for a mother of two boys'."

Regina Brock

Regina Brock Bears

16" linen, mohair *Franklin*.

"I was born in the innocent days of the early 50s where I was raised in and inspired by, the beautiful rural setting of the countryside of Ohio. From the early age of two and a half years I loved to draw! All types of animals were my favorite subjects. I was always encouraged to pursue artistic training, and have fond memories as a child taking weekly instruction in classes at the Cleveland Museum of Art. My formal training came in college and through outside private lessons in painting. I felt my destiny was to offer something artistically of myself to leave to others in the world, and I chose to make teddy bears for all the reasons that they stand for, as a legacy."

Mike and Linda Henry

Bearloom Bears

"We have made some adventuresome career changes over the years, but none has provided as much delight and amusement as creating Bearloom Bears. Linda, a student of Kent State University and the Columbus College of Art and Design, is a freelance commercial artist. Mike, who also attended CCAD and has an extensive training in fine art, design, and cartooning, is an art coordinator for an Ohio-based textbook publisher. Research is an important step in the creation of every Bearloom Bear. Antique journals, historical records and scientific materials on real bears are carefully studied before a new design takes shape. Linda does the majority of the machine work while Mike enjoys giving each bear it's own unique nose. The creative force behind the clothing and accessories is Mike's mother, Barb Henry."

14" acrylic fur *Hareloom*.

Deborah and Derik Hines

Teddy Bear Blessings

"Derik and I started making bears three years ago. I loved the old teddies but knew we couldn't afford them. This motivated me to teach myself to make bears. I loved it and could not stop. Soon bears were all over our house. Many friends encouraged us to take them to shows. Ever since, our life has been full of bears (and babies - we have four girls, four months to six years old). Derik designs our patterns and helps me make the bears in his free time. He's a minister. I'm a full time "Mommy" so our business is in our home."

Wool acrylic *Aaron,* fake fur *Cissie,* wool acrylic *Bethany.*

Sher Masor

The Wicker Buggy

12" nubby cotton fabric *Bertha.*

"With a passion for sewing and collecting fabrics since age ten, I started making dolls 13 years ago, along with a few teddy bears. Finally, seven years ago, the teddy bears took over. I specialize in miniature and one-of-a-kind teddy bears which are produced in very limited numbers and because of this I have chosen to keep my business very small and personal. I moved to Ohio one year ago from Ft. Collins, Colorado, and am so excited to be sharing my creations with collectors in this part of the country!"

5" mohair, short plush *Fuzzy.*

Holly Dyer

5½" alpaca **Bobo**.

7" mohair **Elvin and Melvin**.

"**I** began making terry cloth Paddingtons around 1978 and experimented with various commercial patterns. In 1984 I decided to branch into original bears with my mother, Martha Cramer, drafting patterns and me crafting the bears. Hollybearys came into being. The first bear, the *Watersmith Bear*, was a traditional teddy that was eventually made in seven sizes. The line has expanded into some non-traditional bears. I am now designing some of the bears myself. Perky expressions are a mark of the Hollybearys bear. My husband, Larry, who is a theater manager, and I have two daughters."

Holly Dyer

Vanilla Beanblossom.

10" mohair *Cocoa Beanblossom*.

12" wool *Amos*.

Jackie Morris

8" mohair *Tiny Tim*.

"**I** made my first teddy bear when I sat in on my mother's 4-H group at the age of four years. That was my first sewing project, and since then I have made everything from wedding dresses to a man's suit. I first started making bears to sell at craft shows about two and a half years ago. At the time I thought I was making kids toys, but it didn't take me long to discover the wonderful world of teddy bear collecting. Since then I have grown to love making bears more than anything I have ever done."

Maria Schmidt

The Charlestown Bear

21" mohair *Oliver Fox*.

"I have a B.F.A. from Central Michigan University in Ceramic Sculpture (1979) and started making jointed bears in 1983 in St. Louis, Missouri. I try to capture the look of the early Steiffs. I specialize in big bears, 20" and up, and also love to make Golliwogs — fully jointed. I plan to sell only at shows, featuring "one-of-a-kind" and very limited editions. I have many new projects in the works — including several studio pieces. I make very few bears a year, 50 or less with hopes to double my production next year. I also do museum quality restoration of early Steiffs."

25" mohair *Kodi*.

Maria Schmidt

Group of Schmidt bears.

38" mohair **Ollie**.

Jodi Rankin

Bears by Jodi

14" mohair **Whitley**.

10" mohair **Dustin**.

"**I** am a 33 year old house wife with 2 children, 13 and 3 years old. My husband is a Columbus Police Officer. I just developed into a teddy bear artist this year when the teddy bear bug bit me! I was collecting other peoples bears when I realize I had to start making them for myself. I started giving birth to some really 'fun' teddy bear personalities by designing all my own patterns. Each bear has about five hours of tender loving care put into it. My hopes are that I can design and produce really top quality bears for years to come."

Betsy Hilgendorf

Purple Crayon

10" mohair.

10" mohair.

"**I** was born with a travel bug in my blood, predestined to become a travelling bear artist. In 1979, as a high school Junior, I enrolled in a sewing class. Everyone else chose to make clothing. I wanted to make a bear. That incident was far more significant than I dreamed at the time. I've been making bears ever since. However, it wasn't until 1984 that I figured out a way to combine my desire to travel with my bear making talent. Thus, the birth of Purple Crayon Bear Co., my best excuse yet to travel!"

Rosalie Frischmann

Mill Creek Creations

14" Merino wool *Sweet Ted*.

7" mohair *Birtee the Bellhop*.

"**I** learned to sew at the age of seven. I spent much of my childhood making and designing doll clothes. Eventually, I made and designed many clothes for myself. My bear making career didn't begin until years later. Always having a fondness for bears, I decided they would make the perfect gifts for my young daughters. I wanted them truly special, so I made them myself. What began as gifts for my daughters has turned into a full time business, designing and making collectors bears. My bears are all my original designs. They are made of natural fabrics, many of which are hand-dyed."

Northwest

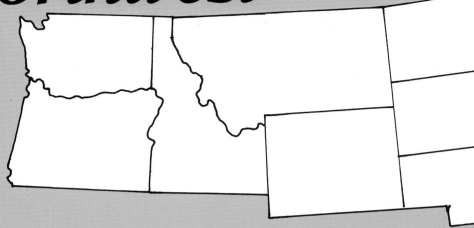

Becky Mannon

Acrylic *Wellington Thurston III*.

"**I** grew up in a small farming community in Western Nebraska. I have always been involved in creating gifts for family and friends. I have always loved working with my hands creating something original. I try to put individuality into each item I create. In 1984 I produced a copywrited original doll, the *Becky Ann Doll*, and had my first experience in marketing. My latest venture *Wellington* has been my favorite project because of the tremendous personality of each bear."

Pam Carlson

10" mohair *Arden*.

"As long as I can remember I have enjoyed designing and creating for home, gifts and sales. One day during a time of physical illness, I decided to make a teddy bear. Soon after I was selling teddies to many stores all over the U.S. I enjoy collecting and decorating with bears and will always appreciate the fun and laughter bears bring to people."

4" *Amy*, 10" *Ashton*, 10" *Addie*, 7" *Alison*, all mohair.

Deanna Duvall and Dayla Smoland

12" mohair *Grand's Bear*.

"Grands' Bear® is the first collaborative project for either Deanna or Dayla. Dayla supplied the idea and Deanna the bear design. The completion of the project was truly a joint effort. Dayla is also a nurse and an aspiring screenwriter. Deanna has been designing bears for over ten years under the logo *My Bears*. Both women are bear collectors who reside in Forest Grove, Oregon, with their families.

12" mohair *Grands Bear*.

Susan Erickson

Rainy Day Bears

7" mohair *Twinkle*.

"After earning a master's degree in literature from the University of Oregon, I taught high school English for 13 years in the Northwest. Three years ago my husband, daughter and I moved to the Oregon coast where I devoted myself to teddy bear making. I love creating bears — each new one seems to have its own personality! I am also an avid collector!"

9" mohair *Loyal Ted*.

Miriam Hertz

Hertzbear

7" mohair *Pixley*.

"I was introduced to the world of teddy bear making and collecting in 1983 while teaching craft sewing classes at a local fabric store. The first bears were made from commercial patterns but I soon started experimenting with my own designs and now make only original bears and their clothing. Bear making is a very time consuming activity in my life but I am lucky to have the wholehearted support and help of my husband and two sons. My bears are fully jointed with ultra-suede paws and German glass eyes. They are almost always dressed or accessorized."

11" mohair *Tristen*.

Hillary Hulen

Heidibears & Heidihares

15" German mohair *Cinnabar*.

Hillary has a degree in Wildlife Biology from Southern Oregon College. She also studied scientific illustration at the Smithsonian in Washington, D.C. She was a biological illustrator for several magazines and she and her husband published a nature newspaper. In 1981, to finance a bird watching trip to Mexico, they made and sold their first basket of bears.

12" German mohair *Yank*.

Lara-Zano

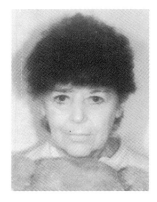

"I am the Lara-Zano originator of Lara-Zano bears and dolls and have a junior partner, Julie, who is my daughter. I make my bears mostly from upholstry fabric but recently have been experimenting with mohair and although I will keep using upholstry, I really love the feel of mohair bears. My bears grow their own personalities and are named and dressed accordingly. I think my greatest pleasure is derived from people that portray their joys received from my bears."

15" mohair *Just Me*.

Julie Lara-Zano II

Lara-Zano

12" upholstery fabric *Old Salty*

"I started collecting bears at a young age and They bring me much happiness. I learned how to make bears at about age 15 when my mother taught this loving craft to me. When people are pleased and enjoy my work, this is my greatest pleasure! My bears vary in size and price from six inches to a foot tall and always carry a companion. They are made from upholstry fabric and dressed in wools and icos. When I see my finished product I smile hoping my bears make other people smile too!"

12" upholstery fabric *Free Puppies*.

Bev Miller Landstra

9½" imitation fur *Ira the Snake charm Bear*.

"My talent for creating teddy bears all started by making teddies for my son. Little did I know it would be something to build a career upon at that time. I now sell my bears coast to coast in speciality bear shops where my motto is: 'teddy bears can do anything or be anyone.' I'm in my seventh year as a teddy bear artist and still love the challenge of making bears. I feel it was such an honor to be one of the first bear artists featured in the first issue of *Teddy Bear and friends*."

10" German mohair *BP Griswald*.

Rose Policky

8" mohair *Longfellow*.

"I made my first miniature bear about five years ago. He hardly resembled a teddy bear though. My son thought it was a kangaroo. With no formal design experience I went through much trial and error to design a bear I liked. Now some 1150 bears later I enjoy making the bears even more then that first one. Each bear is a new surprise with his own facial expression. Best of all, I have found the teddy bear dealers, collectors and artists are some of the most interesting and wonderful people around."

1/2" to 1½" ultrasuede *Itty Bitty Buddies*.

Linda Stafford

Log Cabin Bears

9" Merino wool *Grizzelda* and *Grizwald*.

"With a strong background in art, sewing and crafts, I began designing bears in 1985 when I couldn't find a kit or pattern for an antique-looking teddy. My current line includes 15 different bears, all sewn on my antique treadle sewing machine and finished with several hours of handwork. I place special emphasis on creating bears with sweet, endearing expressions and a hint of a smile. From their humble beginnings here in the woods of Southern Oregon, Log Cabin Bears have become treasured members of collections all across the country."

16" mohair *Kenny*.

Barbara D. Whisnant

Barbear and friends, Ltd.

10" German plush *Little Bear Blue.*

"I have been making teddy bears for nearly three years. *Barbear* came about because of the special qualities I wanted in a bear I could call my own creation. After months of work and some kind suggestions the bear was "born." I have a daughter, a son and a husband who supports and encourages me. I love doing what I am doing."

16" mohair and music box *Jesterbear.*

Doris Beck

Dori's Bears

15" mohair *Rosebud.*

"As a Registered Nurse, I have had a lot of experience with a needle. I can't remember when I didn't sew. I started making bears as toys for porcelain dolls. Gradually I made larger bears and entered them in contests. Friends borrowed my bears for store and window displays. I soon learned there was a market for my creations and in 1985 Dori's Bears and the Couturier Bear® became a real business. The rest is history. I now have bears all over the U.S., in several foreign countries, and some are even doing sea duty with the U.S. Navy!"

19" tipped mohair *J. Pierpont Honeyeater.*

Candy Corvari

Candy Bears

9" mohair, 6" Rayon and 4" mohair.

"**I** began making teddy bears seven years ago when my oldest son was born. I have a design, drafting and graphics background and have always enjoyed sewing. I love the opportunity to stay home with my two boys and create new bears. But most of all I love going to shows and seeing the joy on others faces when they look at my bears. They may not buy but their comments always make it worth the time and effort."

9½" mohair.

Paula Egbert

Teddy Bear Heaven

8" mohair *Orion*, 11" mohair *Bertie*, and 8" wool *Bennie*.

"**I** have always loved doing creative things like photography, quilting, embroidery and sewing. So for me, bear making started as another hobby and has become a passion. I've been making bears for five years now — after the first one I was just hooked. It's so rewarding to work with a plain piece of fur and see a sweet little bear emerge. I once heard that the secret to making beautiful bears is to incorporate the things you love. Since I love horses it seemed natural to put them with bears in limited edition sets. Each of my bears comes with their own painted enamel charm to identify it for years to come."

11" mohair *Bertie*.

Elaine Fujita-Gamble

Fujita-Gamble Teddies

4" mohair *Elaine*.

"**I**'m a full-time physical education specialist here in Edmonds, starting my eleventh year as a teacher. My teddy bear collection was started years ago when a friend bought teddy bears for me as gifts. I now have a nice collection of artist-made bears, antiques, collectible commercial bears. Teddy bear making has always been a hobby for me. Due to my limited production, I only sell my bears at shows, but I do enjoy personally meeting the collectors that buy my bears."

4" plush *String of Hearts*.

John Paul Port

Van Poort & Co.

24" Merino wool *The Starkeeper*.

"**I** am indeed an addicted arctophile. I have been exposed to the wonderful world of dolls, toys and teddy bears since birth. My first bear was given to me by my sister on my arrival home from the hospital. I learned at a young age that teddy bears not only were the best medicine but they represented an integral part of history. I started seriously collecting on my own at age seven and am still on the bear hunt today. I run my toy store, Emily's Cottage, in Bremerton, Washington. It was only natural that I start creating my own artist bears."

8" mohair *Iris*.

Karin & Howard Calvin

Ballard Baines Bears

"Every morning Karin and Howard Calvin watch the birds and squirrels play outside their kitchen window. They live at the base of Mt. Si — near Snoqualmie pass that goes to East Washington. Then they settle down to making the Ballard Baines bears that delight Americans from coast to coast. Karin started bear making as a hobby with two friends in 1979. They would make a bear — take it to lunch — and someone would buy it! When the other two partners tired of the venture in 1982 — along came Howard!"

25" mohair *Flossie*.

16" mohair *Bear and His Friend Grinit*.

Karin & Howard Calvin

25" mohair *Goldsmith*.

Janie Comito

Janie Bear

3½" *Child bear & Teddy*.

"**I** enjoy doing very special one of a kind ladies because it incorporates my collecting and designing interests."

1½" wool *William*.

Jerry & Morgan Jurdan

J & M Uniques

"We began designing and crafting our bears, their clothes, and dragons about four years ago when Jerry was laid off and we decided to start our own business. It was difficult starting out and we have come a long way in four years. We now also design and craft virtually all their accessories from glasses and scepters to wooden tricycles, wagons, desks and much more. We love what we do and this is reflected in the quality and creativity of our work. Small limited editions are a trademark of J & M Uniques as we constantly love to design new things."

17" *Mystic Bear*.

17" *Shaman (Spirit Healer) Bear*.

14" plush *Uncle Homer* and *Aunt Louise*.

11" mohair *Teddy, Teddy Tree*.

Kimberlee Port

"The first teddy bear I made was in 1974, for my parents' Christmas present. Since then I've continued to artistically express myself through my bears. To me there is something wonderous in taking a bit of fabric, some thread, stuffing, a few tools, and creating something uniquely your own which has never been seen before. I'm probably best known for my handsewn, fully jointed, bears under 3". However, I've made larger bears, too, including a 21 inch patchwork bear in 1976."

3½" plush *Bearfly* and 1¼" *Baby Bearfly*.

Beverly Matteson Port

Beverly Port Originals

A doll designer and artist, Beverly Port is recognized as a spokesperson in the world of teddy bears. She is credited by leading authors and publications in the field with the resurgence of bear collecting and is recognized for exploring the aesthetic potential of teddy bears as art objects. Her original soft sculpture creations have been exhibited and sold on Madison Avenue. She is also a columnist in *Teddy Bear and friends*® magazine.

Mechanical Nursemaid and *Baby Brat.*™

17" wool and mohair *Hunny Munny.*™

Beverly Matteson Port

22" mohair *King Heinrich Bearkin*.

24" antique mohair *Raggedy Bear.*™

Joyce T. O'Sullivan

Need Just a Bear

11" mohair *Cranberry*.

"I started collecting bears seven years ago when my mother happened to take a class on how to make fully-jointed teddy bears. That gave us the idea to go into business together, a life-long dream for both of us. The master plan was the first two years my mother would do the major sewing and bring me up-to-speed so that I could go off on my own. I find this business to be very rewarding because something I create from a bolt of fabric causes people great joy. I always amaze myself when the product is finished and the public responds so positively to it. The other reason I love bear making is the association of the wonderfully warm and kind people I have met over the past five years."

17" mohair *Joshua*.

Southwest

Shirley Howey

3" mohair *Holly-Beary*.

I am a native of Urbana, Illinois, and married to Roy (also a bear artist) and have five children and 14 grandchildren. I attended the University of Illinois. I designed and made my own clothes. We moved to Mesa, Arizona, in 1950, and have divided our time between there and California since then. I quilted professionally for a year, and worked as an accountant, retiring to spend more time with Roy whose health had failed, I started making bears in January 1986, specializing in hand-sewn miniatures two to six inches tall. I now call the bears Genesis — A New Beginning."

3½" mohair *Seth*

Barbara Koch

13" mohair *Cassie*.

"**M**y interest in bears came about after the first bear show my daughter and I attended in August 1984. The variety of looks and types of bears amazed me. Within the last two years, I have made several different kinds of bears ranging from *The Flapper* to *Miss Gussie*. My favorite, *Cassie*, has many human characteristics — mostly mine: hands on hips yelling or quiet and shy, all depending on the atmosphere. I am a mother of three and work as a bank teller part time."

Diane Gard

D. G. Enterprises

"Since 1982, I have created whimsical, quizzical-eyed bears with a heart. The use of vintage fabrics for some of my original bears has led to a search for the old and unusual fabrics which have become my trademark. My award-winning bears have found their way across the country and into the most discriminating collections. The heartfelt desire to succeed in this unconventional artistic field makes the name I have chosen, A Bear With a Heart, an ideal description of my creations. The glass heart on the bear's chest is a symbol of the love I bring to my work."

15" vintage cotton fabric **Mrs. Rough Rider** and 15" vintage pierce arrow fabric **Rough Rider**.

17" mohair *Old Beau*.

Carolyn Martin

24" plush *Casey Jones*.

23" plush *Uncle Remus*.

"After two years of hand-crafted dolls, I made my first bear from a commercial pattern. I fell in love with bears and started creating my own originals. Three years later I still wanted something unique. After collecting many photographs of bears and working with leather and fur, my leather face bears came into being. Leather and fur are a natural together. My bears seem to speak of the good time's we've had and it's hard to give them up at times."

Mary Kaye Lee
Bear Lee Making It

12" West-German mohair *Beth*.

"I have been 'into' teddies for 30 years. From 1959 thru 1961 I attended the American Academy of Art in Chicago for my design training. After being art director for two publishing houses in Los Angeles, I moved to Colorado in 1967. My designing continued with needlework. Many of my designs appeared on the covers of *Better Homes & Gardens* publications. I turned my talents to teddy bears in 1978, creating stories and personalities for my bears. I often do presentations at teddy bear conventions with my creation, *Harvey*, the World Famous, Traveling Bear."

7" West German llama, French crystal perfume bottle **Perfume Bottle Bear**.

Wendy Brent
Rose Petal Dolls

24" acrylic **Cinjamin**.

16" German plus **Chelsea**.

"I am a native of California who now lives and creates bears and bunnies in the midst of the beauty of Hawaii. I made my first doll 14 years ago in honor of my daughter. I originated the 'rose petal' dolls and bears — and all of my bears have noses of roses or some other fragrance."

Althea Leistikow

9" mohair *Cinder Teddy*.

"I began my teddy bear artist career in 1984 while living in southern California. My studio is now in Topeka, Kansas, where I and my California cat, Panda, live surrounded by beautiful antiques and hundreds of teddy bears. When I am not designing and creating bears, I travel throughout the country attending conventions and giving workshops and programs. My repertoire of designs has grown to fifty and a number of them have been honored with awards."

24" Merino wool *Sam*.

Carol Martin

cm Bears

12" mohair *Ruth E.*

"I am married to Henry — the other half of cm Bears. We have two sons, Chadwick and Detrick. Having been a kindergarten teacher for over 17 years, I am naturally attracted to children and children's toys. My first teddy came at my fifth Christmas, and love for teddies has been growing ever since. Starting to make teddies first as children's toys — often used in my kindergarten classroom, I now enjoy designing and making collector bears."

15" mohair *Dow*.

Lynn Lumley

Grandma Lynn's Teddy Bears

5½" llama *Dear Little Bear*.

4½" hand dyed llama *Jester*.

"**I** designed my first tiny bears 3½ years ago. Right now they measure 3½" to 6½". My little bears brought with them a security and a hope for my future, I didn't dream I would ever know. I am creating something I just love and I see that love coming back to me in each little face. I think best of all I don't feel alone any more. I am a very very grateful and happy teddy bear artist. I thank God every day for the talent he has given me. I can't imagine doing anything more wonderful than making dear little bears for others to love and cherish as I do."

Mary Frances Baldo

MFB Enterprises

5½" mohair *Gabriel*.

"**I** was born and raised in Colorado but have lived in Houston, Texas, for the past 18 years. I married a mining engineer in 1951 and began to travel the world. We have two sons and a daughter, three grandchildren and have enjoyed creating many handmade toys over the years. The last five years have been devoted only to bears. When my large bears began to overflow the spare bedroom I began to make smaller ones. The encouragement of local bear store owners has been the inspiration for dressing the little bears in every imaginable way."

3" ultrasuede *Clint*.

Sherri Dodson

8" acrylic *Wee T. Pocket Bears*.

"I grew up in California during the 50s and 60s. I experienced some of the best, and most changing, music of our times. Music that still affects me today. I automatically relate a great teddy bear to a great song. Growing up in California also provided the opportunity to display my art work at the Young Artist exhibit at the Los Angeles Museum of Art. I am now living in Deer Park, Texas, with my husband, Jim, and son, James, and continue to tie great teddy bears to great songs."

14" acrylic *Cubby Checkers*.

Judy Hill
Hampton J. Bears

11½" mohair *Rusty*.

"I was born in Washington, D.C. and raised in Northern Virginia. I attended college in Florida and lived in Southern New Jersey before moving to Houston in 1983. I am an animal lover. In the summer of 1986 I began making bears with a Linda Spiegel pattern, and designed my first bear in 1986. I rarely do shows because of a full time job with an oil company."

18" wool *Alvin*.

Carol Loucks
Carolsue Designs

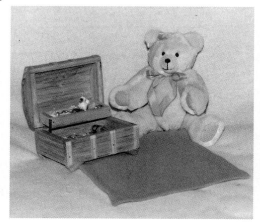

11" acrylic plush *Bubbles*.

"**M**y interest in sewing stuffed animals started twenty-six years ago when I made a set of Winnie the Pooh animals for my niece. My next animals were cats in fairy tale outfits followed by bears and other animals. Many of my designs are custom work — bear outfits for specific events, occupations, sports or companies. In addition to creating bears and costumes I have taught classes in bear making. I tell my students that bear making should be a labor of love and for me it is indeed just that."

18" acrylic plush *Francine*.

Joanne C. Mitchell
Family Tree Bears

16" mohair *Christopher* and *Christine Bearapopolis*.

"**I**'ve been a collector of teddy bears for many years. In 1984 I became a teddy bear artist. In the process, I realized that each one of my bears had become an expression of myself. They not only reflected an ability to create something, but by the grace of God, captured my feelings, moods and daydreams. Somehow I knew that each bear I created would be related and then I decided on the name...Family Tree Bears. Why choose a Family Tree Bear? I have a slogan that hangs in my workroom. It reads, What's a Family Tree Without a Bear?"

16" mohair *Jeffery*.

Mary Neaves

Mama Bear Creations

1⅛" modeling compound **PJ Bear**.

1¼" modeling compound **Peddler Bear**.

"**C**ombining my love for teddy bears and small things, I have created these miniature bears in 1/12th scale. They have been very popular at the miniature shows all over the U.S.A. plus I also sell by mail order. I am an artisan in the International Guild of Miniature Artisans, Ltd. and some of my work is in the Miniature Museums in Dallas and San Diego. Besides the absolute delight I find in creating my teddies, is the joy of seeing the expression on the face of the person when they find that special teddy they cannot live without."

Pam North

Bearing North

13" polyform clay and synthetic fur **Teddy Roosebear**.

12" polyform clay and fur **Balzac**.

"**B**orn in 1943, I have lived in many parts of the United States. While I have received some formal art training, I am basically self-taught. I designed and made my first teddy bear in 1987 in a 24-hour creative binge! My interest in animals extends beyond teddy bears to real-life involvement in wildlife rehabilitation for the past twelve years. I have founded a successful local organization to aid orphaned and injured wildlife. I enjoy photography and produce a line of greeting cards that feature engaging photos of teddy bears."

Carol Pearce

Rosebearys

16" alpaca *Iva Ellen*.

"I began collecting bears in 1984 and making bears in 1986. I combined a full time job in data processing with bear making until early 1988 when I became manager and resident artist of a Houston teddy bear store. Using my maiden name and my family tree, I call my bears Rosebearys with individual bears' names derived from my many family members. My bear, T.J., was chosen for the banquet centerpieces for the 1988 Heart of Texas Show. Rosebearys are very tightly jointed and firmly stuffed, allowing them to stand independently. The Rosebeary trademark: a heart on their sleeve."

8" mohair *T.J.*

JoAnne Adams

S'Bear Change

8" acrylic *Bearnocchio*.

"Gramma Teddy gave me an eight inch doll when I was seven years old. That's when it all began...making dresses and bonnets and panties and shoes and socks and necklaces and tutus and toys and costumes...always playing. Later I was designing and producing clothes, toys, costumes and accessories for children. I moved from California to the high country of Park City, Utah, with my husband and our four children. Inspired by a friend to make teddy bears, I am...making dresses and bonnets and panties and shoes and costumes...always playing...with the great grand child-bearen of Gramma Teddy."

8" acrylic *The Old Bear in the Shoe*.

8" wool *Beardilocks*.

8" acrylic *Bearothy of Oz*.

C. J. Prince

16" mohair *Tiddliewinks*.

"I've been making bears for about eight years. The sizes range from about five inches to 20 inches. Custom bears are a lot of fun to make. I love to take someone's old quilt or coat and turn it in to a teddy bear. I once made a 40 inch bear from an old coat and dressed it in an old wedding gown. I'm a native Texan, born and raised in Dallas. I now reside in Garland, a suburb of Dallas. I've been married for 22 years and have two teenage daughters, whose rooms are full of teddy bears!"

20" mohair *Immy*.

Jan Small

Heirloom Bears

14" German plush *Miss Rosa Honeycake*.

"I've had many careers in my 37 years and my favorite jobs have been: commercial photographer, biology teacher, perfume store owner, and ballet company costume designer. An interest in horticulture and design led me to grad school in Landscape Architecture. I am married to a physician and have a six year old son, Evan. I began making bears in 1985. I love making bears for all the obvious reasons like creating something loveable, working with color, sculpting — but the real fun comes when I've finished a whole hug of bears and they are sitting around smiling back at me."

11" German plush *Cornelius*.

California

Carol Black

Bearhearts

13" alpaca *Baby Maxine*.

The President and *Mrs. Reagan.*

"When discussing the Bearhearts' story in lectures, we frequently make reference to the business as 'a hobby that got carried away.' My background in sales, accounting and business have made very strong contributions, but my creative skills were greatly enhanced by a hobby that started precisely 37½ years ago by a loving father who, through relentless pitching abilities, won a three foot brown plush bear at the Orange County Fair for his first child. Through marriage, three energetic children were conceived and their early years continued to be quite demanding on my time. As they grew into their own independence, less pressures were made which allowed the birth of yet many other new children - The Bearhearts Bears."

Patricia A. Blair

Blair Bears

10" mohair *P. J. Bear*

"I live in Sacramento, California with my husband and two children where I have been making teddy bears since February of 1984. It was a handmade teddy bear, made by my mother, that got me started making bears. I loved the little teddy bear so much, that I wanted another. After all, if Mom could do it, so could I! I borrowed her store bought pattern and made my first bear. It didn't take long before I was designing my own patterns. Thus, a teddy bear artist was born! Each Blair Bear is entirely made by me, from cutting out the bear to stuffing the finished product. All my bears are my own design. It is a great thrill to design an original unique teddy bear. I love each bear for the challenge it has given me."

17" mohair *Humphrey*.

Deanna Brittsan

13" mohair *Duck Soup*.

13" mohair *Kris Bringle*.

"In 1981 I made my first teddy bear. I was reading a magazine and came across a teddy bear pattern, so I said to myself 'why not'? I've sewn many other things — why not make a teddy bear! So I did, and it was not perfect, but I enjoyed making my first bear. I really wanted to improve and get good at this, so I went to a teddy bear show. After months of practicing and observing, I designed my own pattern and put together my first bear. I received a lot of complements from friends and family members. I took their advice and showed my bears to a shop in town. The owner loved them and bought them all! I was surprised and overwhelmed — this was definitely going to be some hobby!"

Barbara Brown

Barbara's Bears

16" acrylic *Rasbeary*.

"I have been making bears for four years at my home in Pasadena. My husband and I have raised three (now adult) children, and after more than 20 years of being a day care mother, I am planning on retiring to spend more time with my bears. At this time I love selling my bears in the Southern California area, at bear sales and conventions. My bears are usually one of a kind, especially if dressed, each outfit is different. I make each bear as if making it for myself. Duplicating is not fun for me, and fun is what my bear making is all about."

16" acrylic *Emily*

Corla Cubillas

14" mohair *Heywood*.

"**I** own *The Dancing Needle* and have been designing and creating teddy bears since 1983. Being a teddy bear artist, I feel I have the best of all worlds. I have been able to develop a rewarding business which has enabled me to be at home and raise my children while at the same time giving me the freedom to express my creative talents. As an award winning artist, I feel that each work of art is a true labor of love. I take a great deal of pride in each bear that comes to life in hopes that one day it will become a well loved antique collectible."

12" wool *Katie*, 12" wool *Brandon*.

Liz Dahle

28" mohair *Tiger*.

"**I**'ve loved teddy bears since I was a little girl. and collected them for years. I especially love the old fashioned teddies with the long arms and sweet shoe button eyes. They inspired me with their wonderful expressions to start so I design my own patterns. I lovingly sew each bear completely by hand making sure each teddy has his own loving expression and personality. Teddy bears will always be a part of me because they give me so much happiness."

21" Merino wool *Teddy*.

Suzanne De Pee

20" mohair *Antoinette.*

"The first Honeypot Bears™ were created in 1983. Almost simultaneously, I felt the need to venture into a real business on my own, and very early into that venture I decided that I not only wanted to create my own original teddies, but also promote those of other talented bear makers I had recently become acquainted with. Thus, the beginning of my very specialized mail order business. I feel fortunate in having worked with, and in making lifetime friends of, so many delightful and creative people during this time in my life, and anticipate continuation with what I am doing for many years to come."

9" synthetic fur *Baby Heidi.*

Denise Dewire

Bearish Delights

13" *Evan*, 9" *Petie*, Merino wool.

"I started making bears in 1985. Since then I have made over 1300 bears and rabbits. Using commercial patterns in the beginning, I soon started designing my own ideas. Using German and English mohair, I create bears from six to 25 inches tall. I dress bears as jesters, sailors and country kids! My bears have won numerous awards."

14" mohair *Spenser.*

Barbara Burbeck

Barbara Burbeck & Bears

19" acrylic *Yancy Lee*.

Barbara Burbeck

"**I** began collecting teddy bears ten years ago. At about the same time I started making bears I designed to give to friends and children. I have won many awards. My bears are known for their bright colors and unusual furs."

21" acrylic *Sophia De Lacey*.

Tatum Egelin

17" vintage fabric *Almetria*.

"**I** started making bears about four years ago. The first one I made as a gift for my grandson. My hobby for many years has been collecting vintage fabric (clothes, quilts, laces). I used my collection to make bears and clothes. I have located vintage fur fabric and wool felt in old warehouses, garages, etc. It is a never ending treasure hunt. Most bears are still made of vintage fabric, although I do use some new fabric. I make all my patterns. I live with my husband, Bill, in an historical area of Los Angeles."

17" vintage fabric *Coconut*.

Flore Emory

Emory-Flore Bears

15" mohair *Little Brother*.

22" *Walley*, 17" *Cody*, 15" *Scott*, mohair.

"About 12 years ago my husband, Neil, and I decided to move from the city to the country. I loved the country life but needed something to keep me busy. I started making teddies for my younger grandchildren and I was off on a most enjoyable hobby. I love to see my little teddies come to be. I like meeting my collectors, bear lovers and fellow bear artists. My bears and dream home has appeared on Hallmark cards and in *Country Living* magazine."

Flore Emory

28" mohair **Nana Bear**.

22" plush **Janette**.

Sandy Fleming

Sandy Fleming Teddy Bears

9" mohair **Peggy Lee, Reuben** and **Robert E. Lee**.

"I took a teddy bear making class in a local craft shop about three years ago. The next day I made two more bears and I was hooked. Not long afterwards I was adapting patterns and finally designing my own patterns, start to finish. I have a strong background in creative arts including painting, drawing, sewing, doll making and quilting. I teach bear making now in the same shop where I got my start. Quality control is extremely important to me. I have won many ribbons for my designs and enjoy doing teddy bear shows and going to conferences."

14" Merino wool **Annabelle**, 4½" mohair **Small Bear**.

Jean Gadano and Mitzi Fry
Tabby's Bears

9" mohair *May Beary*.

Tabby's Bears, a division of Tabby Handworks, which began in 1984, is a mother - daughter partnership. The business is named after Jean Gadano's (mother) two cats and a cat she designed and made to look after the bears in order to keep them out of mischief. The business is based in San Jose, California. Jean does the buying of fur and supplies, and she designs and makes most of the bears. She also does all the photography of the teddy bears. Mitzi Fry (daughter) also has a hand in creating. She makes all the clothes and accessories for the bears. She also takes care of the business details for Tabby Handworks. When needed she stuffs and sews teddy bear arms and legs.

11" *Professor,* 9" *Granny*, 9" *May Beary*, 9" *Wally Beary*, mohair.

Shirley Gibbard and Evelyn Perrine
Teddy Bears on Parade

"We started Teddy Bears on Parade approximately eight years ago. During our friendship that began in 1970, we experimented with a variety of crafts, mainly to be given as gifts. One day we made a bear! We gave bears to friends and relatives, and eventually participated in craft shows. Each bear is a joint effort; we each have our favorite part of the bear making process. Our bears range in size from two inches to four feet tall, all mostly jointed and made from a variety of materials. We wholesale to several stores and enjoy the personal contact that bear shows provide."

26" plush *Chester with friend*.

Serieta Harrell

14" mohair *Beddy-Bye Teddy*.

"After working as head designer for a major manufacturer, the love and the lure of the teddy bear and the desire for more creative freedom, led me to devote my talent to my own business. Sersha bears are prized for their distinct and expressive faces that have all kinds of personality. Many coveted first place awards at major competitions have been won by my bears. But just knowing my creations are loved by collectors is the best award of all. All bears, bunnies, and kittens are exclusively made by myself, making each one a unique and loveable treasure to own."

18" *Annie*, 21" *Lauren*, 18" *Nibletts*, mohair.

Donna Hodges

The Bearons of La Jolla

16" mohair *William and Rebecca*.

"I began designing and making teddy bears after selling two family-owned educational toy shops in San Diego in 1984. I had a desire to remain in the retail business, and since I had a growing interest in teddy bear collecting, became a dealer in teddy bear shows, thus the existence of The Bearons of La Jolla. My direction turned toward artist bears and eventually the design and production of my own bears. I enjoy creating new designs and use only the finest materials available."

7½", 6½", 4½" llama *Goldilocks and the Three Bears*.

Lori Gardiner

Echoes of the Past

"I've been designing and producing teddy bears for about ten years, and recently I added two bunnies to the line. After all these years I still enjoy the challenge of bringing an idea to life. So many times I have needed to immerse myself in a project and bear making fills my day with activity and it also brings a great satisfaction to see my creations so well received by the teddy bear collectors. After all, how many people get to do just what they enjoy — daily!"

16" mohair *Baroness Von Hassenpfeffer*.

16" acrylic fur *Rajah of Bearpoor*.

Lori Gardiner

Madame Butterfly.

10" mohair *Sherman*.

Beth Diane Hogan

"I made friends and other wonderful treasures out of felt as a youngster. As I matured, the materials I used became more expensive. I was still making friends; only now they were monsters and beasts. Often they would scare me so I would add a baby. How could a mother be scary? Now, when it's late at night and everyone else is asleep, I sit creating little bears. For a long time, I only sculpted my miniatures from low-fired clay, but, recently I have begun to sew them too. I'm glad to be able to make friends for everyone."

4" Low Fire Clay *Sewing Bears*.

3" mohair *Bears on Wheels*.

Ann Inman

Annemade

12", 20" mohair *Hunny Bears*.

"Annemade Bears started about five years ago at a local craft store. I started with a simple pattern and eventually developed my own line of artist bears. The newest bears are a line of mechanical bears that are unique to the artist bear world. The mechanicals have become the most fun to design and produce. Every new piece is very much an individual. With a family of five children I am sometimes amazed I get anything done. I attribute it to a great love for what I am doing. Life at my house is very busy and never dull."

11" mohair *Lady Bears*.

Pat Johnson

PJ Bears

30" mohair *Chester*.

"A life of education, training and practical experience has given me the confidence to become a teddy bear artist and doctor. My education gave me the foundation to create with fabrics. In 1983 it came together as I started my business, PJ Bears. As I became known as a bear artist many requested me to repair bears and that became the major portion of my business. These tasks progressed from repair to restore to resurrect to reincarnation: repair — mend and clean, restore — replace worn parts, resurrect — put together bears torn apart by pets and jealous lovers, reincarnation — totally remaking the bear using the bear parts as a pattern."

24" mohair *Wayne*.

Doris King

Doris King Originals

11" mohair *Sarah*.

"**A**fter years of making clothing for my children, I made my first teddy bear in early 1983. I showed it to a friend who owned a shop. She asked for several, which I made, and its been go — go — go ever since. The teddy bear business has been very good to me. It has given me the opportunity to design and create. I've met so many great people at the shows and conventions I have attended. I've been so pleased with the way my bears have been accepted. My husband, Dennis, and I have raised six children and are now enjoying our grandchildren (eighteen so far)."

15" synthetic fur *Nancy Jane*.

Barbara King

17" mohair *Rosemary* and *Roseanne*.

"**B**ears came into my life on January 30, 1987, when I attended a class on how to make a jointed teddy bear. Since that day my life has not been the same. I used to do lots of sewing for myself, daughters and grandchildren, but that was BB (before bears). I also did years of crafts, quilting and boutiques, but that was BB. My favorite time is when the bear is finished and it looks up as if to say 'I love you and thanks for bringing me to life'."

18" synthetic fur *Crystal*.

Sharon Lapointe

16" *Christopher*, 14" *Corey* mohair.

"I have always loved teddy bears, but it was in 1982 that I made my first jointed bear. Then I knew I had found my creative nitch. Soon after I began designing my own patterns. The inspiration for my first design came from my father's first teddy, which has played with three generations of children in our family. He now sits at my house watching over all the newer, less-experienced bears. Since then the world of bears has been a great learning experience, and has given me the opportunity to travel and meet lots of wonderful people with the same love of bears."

16" *Hildic*, 10" *Heidi* mohair.

Wendy Lockwood
Country and Bears

16" *Nutmeg*, 11" *Lambchops* mohair.

"I've been making bears for four years and loving every minute of it. I get to work out of my house, travel, and be my own boss. I've also made some wonderful friends. I have a clothing, textiles and business degree — so it's only natural that I'd find a way to combine this background into a business — and it worked! This is a family business with my husband doing a lot of the jointing and most of the stuffing. I do the designing and sewing."

19" synthetic fur *Scruff*.

Beverly Mark
The Cubby Hole

5½" mohair *Buddy Bears*.

21" mohair *Mt. Charlie* and *Emmy Lou*.

"I have been designing bears, teaching bear making, repairing old bears, writing about bears and painting bears for six years. Although I have seriously thought about quitting many times, I seem to be addicted to all furry things that hold my heart. I am expecting to have a great surprise ready for the new year!"

Cindy Martin

37" wool
(One of a kind) Sailor Yesterbear.

"A native Californian, I live in Fresno with my husband, Gary, and daughters, Wendy and Cory. I love the designs and workmanship of old things. Admiration for beautiful antique bears led me to design a small button-jointed bear for my daughters in 1982. Now there are at least thirty-eight designs of 'Yesterbears' ranging in size from 3¼" to 54". I try very hard to make each one a unique character. The individual that finally emerges is always a surprise to me. Nothing pleases me more than hearing that someone has gotten pleasure from one of my bears."

24" mohair *Soft Yesterbear*.

Judi Maddigan

"My articles appear in many teddy bear publications, and my designs have won national awards. In addition to producing original bears for collectors, I teach bear making for all levels. I received a B.A. in Art from U.C. Berkeley. I live with my husband and teenaged daughter in San Jose, California. All my bears after number 100 are marked at the top center back with a riveted, tooled leather circle: © Judi Maddigan, No. ___."

16" synthetic plush *Bearly Adequate*.

I want a hug

Judi Maddigan

11" **Chubby Cubby**, 15" **Cubby Cousins** synthetic fur.

Karine Masterson

13" acrylic **Nutmeg**.

14" acrylic **Ashley Bluebearrie**.

"It's difficult to remember that two years ago I was a costume designer and bears were not part of my life. I was kind of thrown into this enchanted world by mysterious forces and that now they give me so much enjoyment and the opportunity of working at home with my 3 year old daughter Sara who helps pack the bears for shipping. That has been the greatest gift of beardom, my time with Sara and my husband Rick. I have never missed costuming because I now design bears and their clothes. You see I won't sell a naked bear."

Barbara McConnell

McB Bears

24" *Papa Bear*, 21" *Mama Bear*, 11" *Baby Bear*, wool-mohair blend.

19" mohair *Whitney and Wendy go to School*.

"I am married and the mother of two children and reside in Escondido, California. My studio is in my home where I design and create my bears and dolls. After attending my first teddy bear show in April, 1986, I decided to 'go for it' and establish my own teddy bear business. My desire was to have teddy bears designed with clothing that represented classic values of America. I hope that others will experience a great deal of love from my teddy bears and that they will also bring collectors a tremendous amount of joy and happiness."

Flora Mediate

Flora's Teddys

18½" alpaca *Ted E. Bear*.

15" acrylic *Spock Bear*.

"A teacher of art for over eight years, I began making toys after the birth of my child. I created my first bear in 1981 at the request of a shop owner in which my designs were being sold. The shop owner decided to use a teddy bear theme for Christmas and this first 'child' was the beginning of a most productive avocation. Recognition of my capabilities has come in the form of many awards."

Sue Newlin

Sue Newlin Collectibles

22" synthetic fur *Savanah*.

"**M**y adventure into bear making began in 1982. While my designs vary in size and style, they continue to maintain that look of sweet innocence for which they have been known. Since the first National A.T.B.A.G. Convention in 1985, I have increased my travels each year to include many bear shows throughout the country. In May 1988 I had the honor of being invited to Japan to help celebrate the fourth anniversary of the Cuddly Brown teddy bear shops. While there, I was given the opportunity to teach a bear making class and give in-store demonstrations. Wherever I have traveled my bears have been a delight to the young at heart."

15" Merino wool *Zoe*.

18" acrylic *Pink Bear*.

Penny Noble

"**I** have been creating bears for about six years now and have been encouraged constantly by Kim and René, owners of Earth Bound Bear & the Hare. I've made so many different ones, I've lost count. I continue to enjoy the making of the bears as it seems like there is always a new idea around the corner. The bears faces are the most important step for me, as the placement of the nose, mouth and eyes can change the whole idea of the bear. Each of my bears wears a miniature penny around its neck, my signature."

14" acrylic *Milo*.

Kaylee Nilan

Beaver Valley

"I have always loved sewing and designing, though, I never dreamed that I would be making a living at it. Trained as a Flight Instructor and a Commercial Helicopter Pilot, the advent of children and single parenthood required a change of occupation. We live in such a glorious place. It is secluded, peaceful and wild. As I cast about for a direction, I knew I wanted to make something that grew from this place, and was connected to the life here. Then the Jack Rabitts, Beavers, Bears, and Mtn. Lions came into being and Beaver Valley was born."

22" plush *Meri*.

36" plush *Francis*.

Kaylee Nilan

36" plush *Three Sisters*.

Cat Orlando

10" synthetic fur *Brandilee*.

17" mohair *My Honey*.

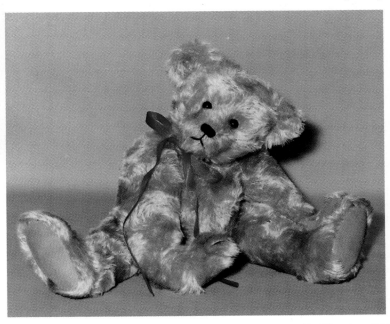

"I have been sewing since the age of five thanks to the many talents of my mother and my grandparents. I had made bears for my children when they were young but it wasn't until July 1986 that my friend encouraged me to try a jointed bear. Obviously I loved it! I now create original designs and have inspired my daughter to do the same. With the help and support of my family, I travel to bear shows where I enjoy placing my bears in new homes. Just knowing that your bears make people smile is a truly rewarding feeling!"

Mac Pohlen

13" mohair *PeeDee* and *HiDee.*

"Since 1985, the days I am not in my workroom creating bears have become rare. Frankly, there's nothing I would rather be doing. While my bear designs have evolved after the years, there is a certain 'look' that has carried through each stage of growth. Consistency, quality and attention to detail have always marked my bears. It's difficult being a perfectionist. My greatest joy is seeing bear people channel their extra love through one of my bears."

Robert Raikes

Robert Raikes Collectibles by Applause

Train Engineer.

"Many people ask me how did I get into making teddy bears. There are really two stories that answer that question. My early sculpture, that included human figures, birds and animals led me to doing art dolls and from these I developed the bears and all their friends. But there is another story: the love for my fellow human beings and what I could do to help make this a more loving and caring world. I've believed from my youth that God has given all of us our own creativity. For me there is a great deal of satisfaction knowing there are thousands of people throughout this world that own Raikes originals."

Robert Raikes

Cowboy Bears.

Gloria Rosenbaum

Rosenbear Designs, Ltd.

"One thing that we have tried to do with Rosenbears Designs is to try to bridge the enormous gap existing between teddy bear collectors and doll enthusiasts. We've tried to develop an extravagant teddy bear to enthuse both types of collectors. We offer a traditional teddy bear but our forte is in our extravagant imagination."

16" mohair *Vicki Rosenbear*, 16" acrylic *Ashley Rosenbear*, 10" mohair *Sara Rosenbear*.

24" mohair *Barney Rosenbear*, 21" mohair *Rhett Rosenbear*, 24" mohair *Max Rosenbear*.

15" mohair *Casey and his Cow*, 15" mohair *Peggy and her Pig*.

Laurie Sasaki

The Bearrie Patch

5" mohair *Bear Band*.

2½" mohair *Muzzle Bears*.

"It's hard to imagine a job more ideal for me than my own: teddy bear maker! I've been making bears full time for three years now (since 1985), and I still wake up each morning eager to get started with my work. I've never had any formal art or design training, but I've dabbled in a variety of crafts, teaching myself from books and through experimentation everything from basketry to papier mâché puppet making to china painting, etc. However, the most useful by far are the skills I learned from my mother, an accomplished needlewoman. She taught me, as a child, the rudiments of designing patterns, hand and machine sewing and embroidery."

Denis Shaw

Denis's Den

11" synthetic fur *Toca*.

12" synthetic fur and upholstery materials *Astri*.

"I learned to make a teddy bear from a friend. My first animals became gifts and raffle items to raise money for local causes. Although I studied printmaking, illustration and photography (in Europe and the San Francisco Art Institute), and worked in crafts, making animals seemed the most rewarding. I am a lover of wildlife and enjoy nature in all its aspects. I have studied animals in the national parks of East Africa...in the zoo, the park, or the woods. My fun comes from designing a new pattern. Besides my many furry woodland creatures, I have created a group of imaginary endangered species from another planet seeking refuge on earth."

Linda Spiegel

Bearly There, Inc.

"My creation *Gus* changed the shape of the bear world, according to some of my peers. I have been designing dolls and bears for friends and church groups for over fifteen years. A mother of six, and a grandmother of two, I started Bearly There in my garage with $150. and lots of faith and hope! My bears are now sold all across America, and in Japan, Canada and Australia!"

13" synthetic fur *Lizzee*.

Linda Spiegel

14" synthetic fabric ***Boy Bear***.

15" synthetic fur ***Homer***.

14" mohair ***Old Bear***.

Colleen Tipton

Collee Bears

8" mohair.

20" (far left), 12" (center front), 12" (center back), 15" (far right), 8" (back left), 8" (back right), all mohair.

"**M**y love of bears first started when my parents, Wally and Linda Mullins started me collecting about 1976. I actually attempted my first handmade bear about 1980, and have been producing different designs ever since. I have kept it a small business so that I may work at home, and be with my family. My son Loren has helped me create many of the characters and I've titled them, using family names. It has been a treasured experience!"

Joan Woessner

Bear Elegance

18" synthetic fur *Teddy Goodbar*.

"**I** began Bear Elegance in June, 1986, with the support and aid of my husband, Mike. In October of that same year I began my unique line of bears called 'Tumble Bears.' These cuties are especially loveable because they can be posed in various positions that best show-off their personalities. My bears have detailed faces with personalized expressions and the touch of mink at the eyelashes. My use of German glass eyes and quality materials ensure that each and every fully jointed bear will delight for years to come."

11½" mohair **Cinnamon**.

13½" Merino wool **Jeffrey**.

12" mohair **Carmel**.

Paulette Tucker

Tucker Teddies

14" mohair *Punkin*.

14" acrylic fur ***Ted***.

"I live in San Jose, California, with my husband and five children. Since I was a child, teddy bears have been the love of my life. My world changed several yars ago when I took a bear making class. It was magic to see a cuddly bear emerge from a simple piece of fur. I was hooked! That is when Tucker Teddies was born. I love designing bears. It's very exciting to start with a concept and see it take form and come alive. I stitch a little love into each teddy. The most enjoyable part of making bears is seeing the joy that they bring to other people's lives."

Beverly Wright

Wright Designs

15" mohair ***Santa***.

"I grew up in a home where the sewing machine was always set up, and my mother encouraged me to sew and knit. As a student I majored in art, also studied dressmaking, weaving, metal sculpture, mosaics, and practically lived in San Francisco's art galleries. I made my first jointed bear in 1980, and 2,400 bears since then. My proudest accomplishment is having raised a son and two daughters. My favorite pastimes are playing with grandchildren, and quilt making. Quilts are on my beds and walls, and on the small beds of the bears who live with me."

Other *Countries*

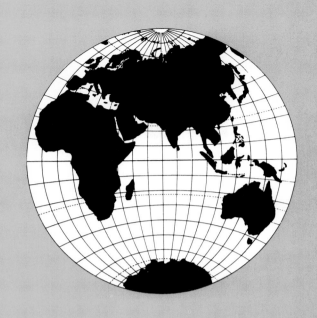

Heather Brook

Bearly Collectable Bears
Australia

"**F**or many years I've collected baby dolls and made cloth dolls and soft toys while always being very interested in bears. My introduction to bear collecting and bear making only started about 3½ years ago. My theory is what can be done with a cloth doll you can do with a bear when making it. I greatly enjoy making and dressing my bears especially the baby and child-like bears, and will continue for as long as they bring pleasure to others and myself."

23" acrylic **Burly Bertha**.

18" acrylic **Baby Nicholas Bearly**.

Marjory Fainges

Australia

9" suede cloth **Edward**.

"**B**eing the owner, custodian of over 500 modern, old and antique teddies in my Doll & Toy Museum in Brisbane, Australia, I naturally wanted to make my own bears. Several years ago I started making speciality bears and have won prizes with them in New South Wales, South Australia and Queensland. Two years ago I was asked to teach the art of jointed teddy bears at Brisbane's Colleges of Technical and Further Education. Having a wry sense of humour my bears develop personalities of their own."

16" acrylic **Teddy R**.

Anne Keane

Anne Keane Dolls
Australia

18½" porcelain **Garrump**.

"**I** was born in Tasmania, Australia, in 1940 and have a background in commercial art, silk screening, painting and sculpting. I discovered doll making in the late 1970s and became a doll artisan in 1984. I progressed to original works, beginning with *Blinky Bill* (Koala) and securing further world rights to Australian characters from childrens books and my own originals concentrating on the Australian theme."

9½" porcelain **Blinky Bill**.

Gerry Warlow

Australia

"I live with my husband and two teenage children in the small country town of Rosewood in Queensland, Australia. My first efforts in bear making were in 1983, eventually I overcame my fears of those dreaded joints and many new and original designs have since been created. I find nothing more rewarding then seeing a new design come to life."

17" fabric *Veteran Bears*.

Cathy Hamilton

Canada

5½" mohair *Rosey*.

5½" mohair *Dennis*, 5½" mohair *Dominick*.

"Involved in crafts all my life, I started making bears and bear related items several years ago. Since graduating from university, I have been employed by a municipal government as an archivist, restricting my bear making to a part-time vocation. My painted boxes, sculpted figures, and fully-jointed mohair bears are designed and made with care. As I make a bear, I am convinced it develops a particular personality. There are times I wish I could keep every bear I make, but I've run out of space!"

Dawn Nicholl

New Zealand

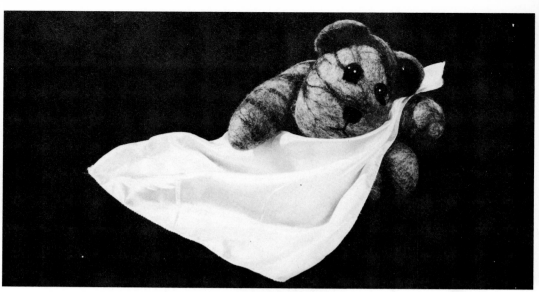

9" wool *Shy Sue*.

"**M**arried with four children I was born, raised and have spent most of my life in the north of New Zealand. Over the years I have experimented with art and design in various forms. Painting, sculpture, pottery and fibre arts. Also for many years I have collected dolls and toys. During a period of working with felt in sculptural form the two things came together and I evolved my own distinctive individually hand molded felt bears. I now have nineteen different characters, with more developing all the time."

12½" wool *Sh! Sh! Shoulder Bear*.

Dawn Nicholl

8½" wool *Possibility Bear*.

Joyce and Barry C. Church

England

The Old Fashioned Teddy Bear Company

14" mohair *Mummy*, 10" mohair *Baby*, 17" mohair *Dad*.

"The Old Fashioned Teddy Bear Company was launched in the spring of 1987 by Joyce and Barry Church with the aim of producing traditional, fully jointed, mohair teddy bears for the collector. Prior to this Joyce had had an interest in making soft toys purely for her own enjoyment. Encouraged by friends in 1985 she decided to turn this interest into a business and started producing toys to order. 1986 saw the start of a new phase towards jointed teddy bears. Joined by her husband Barry in 1987 they relaunched themselves under their "new" Old Fashioned name."

Gail Everett

England

14" *Country Lady*.

"Gail Everett, 29, lives in Newton Poppleford and works as a graphic designer at Tony Corbett Advertising in Exmouth. She made her first bears for her brother, Paul, when he was little, but didn't start her own bear brigade until 1985. Since then she has designed over 50 bears — many of them as one-off specials.

14" *Beardica*.

16" fur fabric *Huntley*.

Susan Rixon

Nonsuch Teddies
England

"I was born at Cheam in Surrey near the site of King Henry VIII's Nonsuch Palace which provided the name for my small company, started in 1978. From small beginnings an exclusive range of teddy bears have been carefully designed for both children and serious collectors worldwide. My speciality being very small limited editions with signed and numbered certificates. I am married to David who has joined me in what is now a very full time occupation for both of us. We have two sons and live near Reading in the Royal County of Berkshire."

18" mohair *Wessex*.

David Wright

England

12" mohair *Effie*.

"I am 28, and have been designing and making bears since 1986, inspired by my wife's childhood bear, and a need to create 'Real Bears'. I generally buy fabrics in small quantities as I find a colour or texture which says, 'Please make me into a Bear!' From the start I decided to make each bear a different combination of material and design. With so many possible fabrics to be found, plus hand-dyeing, why not make each bear unique? Each bear is an individual to me and we work together from first snip to last stitch."

20" mohair *Archie*.

Elke Kraus

West Germany

"I was born in 1941 in East Germany and had no toys. My longing for toys increased and that is why I began to collect dolls and teddy bears. One day I made a teddy for my son John (11 years old) and people liked the teddy so much that I had to make more and more, including some for the customers of my teddy bear clinic (hospital)."

20" mohair *Franz*.

Artists' Index

Provided is an alphabetical list of artists within the book. For an index organized geographically, please see the introductory page of each geographical section. Addresses were accurate as of completion of the manuscript. Many teddy bear artists work out of their homes and as such do not encourage walk-in business. Please write to artists to ascertain how you can see their complete range of designs or add their hallmark designs shown in the first *Teddy Bear Artist's Annual*.